Bonsai Kids

Debbie,

Life is an adventure.

Peace,

Steve

Spring 2022

BONSAI KIDS

Stephen Ling
Author of
For My Hands Only
Crazy Americans
Speaking English vols. 1 and 2
Growing up Chinese
This Is China
Prodigal Son
Letter to Fellow Immigrants: A Memoir

Bonsai Kids

A Must-Read

Dr. Xianfeng Zhou, Hamamatsu University
School of Medicine, Japan

Stephen E. Ling

Library of Congress Control Number: 2022900633
ISBN: Hardcover   978-1-6698-0669-1
               Softcover   978-1-6698-0668-4
               eBook   978-1-6698-0667-7

Print information available on the last page.

Rev. date: 01/13/2022

To order additional copies of this book, contact:
Xlibris
844-714-8691
www.Xlibris.com
Orders@Xlibris.com
833815

To
Jay Qi-long Han,
Michael Qiao Jia,
Duan Xi,
Chao Chen,
Minwei Ai,
Ryan Jiaxin Shen,
Shouheng Deng,
Aaron Sun Min,
Mu Yuan,
Jady Xianfeng Zhou,
Roy Qi Cai,
Ruby Wei You,
Zoey Tienfeng Zuo,
Jake Chen,
Martial Jieheng Yang,
Allen Chen,
and many other bonsai kids who have shared their life
stories with me when I was a visiting professor in China.

INTRODUCTION

One summer back home in Washington State, during my vacation break as a visiting professor teaching in mainland China, I decided to visit the Pacific Bonsai Museum, located a short distance from my residence. Actually, I had a student guest from mainland China with me who, at the time, was planning to pursue a PhD in integrated biology in America. The trip to the bonsai museum was my idea, hoping to expose him to the American version of the bonsai culture. That was my plan.

The museum offered traditional and contemporary bonsai exhibits featuring world-class bonsai from the Pacific Rim countries: the USA, Canada, China, Japan, and Korea. Though usually associated with Japan and Zen Buddhism, some Chinese families of my students in mainland China had told me bonsai tree cultivation actually originated in China, not Japan. I wasn't prepared for this revelation and surprise. Bonsai is actually an art that has existed in Asia for centuries.

They had also informed me that *penjing* or *penzai* is an ancient Chinese art of creating artistically cultivated trees and landscapes in miniature. In China, you can see classical Chinese gardens in well-preserved pre-1949 houses of the rich and famous (the formation of communist China in 1949 forever changed its social, economic, and cultural landscape) with arrangements of miniature trees and rockeries known as *penjing*. This artistic arrangement of carefully pruned trees and rocks, referred to as "living sculptures" or as "three-dimensional poetry" in China, captures the spirit of nature, producing natural sceneries in small pots, essentially small-scale versions of special trees and natural landscapes. The bronze container or *pen* originated in Neolithic China and was used in court ceremonies and religious rituals in ancient China.

My student guest was not the least intrigued nor impressed with the American display of bonsai trees. Obviously, he had seen superior and better displays in his own country. However, I did learn that growing or nurturing bonsai trees is for the rich, serious, or professional gardeners both in China and the USA. What I experienced that day of the elegant potted plants at the museum was a series of images flashing in my mind of how serious gardeners would take the necessary time, money, knowledge, experience, and patience to cultivate a bonsai tree. The words *commitment* and *devotion* in pursuit of bonsai came to mind.

I had the privilege to attend some classes, for a purpose, on how to grow bonsai trees. I might want to teach Chinese students in mainland China how to raise and take care of bonsai trees. Why not? It's to fill a void or have some leisure time or avoid boredom.

I did that with introducing the Chinese mah-jongg to my Chinese students. While I was in mainland China, I taught (as an American or outsider) some Chinese students how to play the famous mah-jongg, a tile game once developed in late 1800s around the Yangtze River delta in mainland China. It would spread its popularity to cosmopolitan cities like Shanghai and Beijing. American tourists and businessmen would adopt it and carry it back to the USA. It is a gin-rummy-like game played with tiles and not cards. It has become a popular American pastime since it was introduced to Americans in the early 1920s.

In fact, I was introduced to mah-jongg by a young American couple, my first host family, when I first came to the USA to study at an

American university in Dallas, Texas. I did not learn it from fellow Chinese, though I was exposed to it when I was a little boy growing up in a Chinese village many moons ago. Not far from our village house in Malaya, there was a grocery store and a coffee shop where men, mostly uneducated farmers, would gather to play mah-jongg all night long until the wee hours in the morning; their loud voices—cursing, losing, or winning—would drift like smoke to my house in the stillness and quiet of the night. To the many Christians in the village, mah-jongg was for gamblers and sinners. To the village men, mah-jongg gave them a chance to mingle with other farmers in the village; and also, it was the only source of pleasure in an isolated village of mostly pigs and rubber trees, the chief source of income for many of them. Almost everyone eked out a living from the soil. All the residents in this village shared the same destiny—subsistence survival. And mah-jongg gave them some relief and pleasure.

In China, many Chinese parents are against their children coming close to mah-jongg (the game is usually played with money, associated with gambling, once banned by the communist government), though many of them are addicted to it, like how the modern youth is completely taken over or consumed by computer games. I did it for a simple reason—to activate their brain and also to give the students a chance to socialize with other students from different departments in the campus. Only curious or outgoing and ambitious students who befriended me were invited to a dinner, followed by a mah-jongg game in the privacy of my apartment. We did this at the beginning of a semester when students were less busy with their studies and piles of homework.

So in my mind, I could also teach them how to grow a bonsai tree as part of their extracurricular activities in addition to their obsession with playing basketball or watching a Japanese porn movie. Life as a bonsai kid could be very boring in the campus or in any part of mainland China unless you were born with a silver spoon in your mouth. Other than different student clubs or organizations in the campus and studies, there were not much of anything else to occupy their limited leisure time or compete for their attention.

In my first introductory bonsai class in the USA, we learned to select a species or tree that is indigenous to where we live and decide whether you want to grow it indoor or outdoor. Basically, one is faced with three choices when choosing a tree: (1) deciduous ones, like crab apple trees and Japanese or Chinese elms; (2) coniferous ones, like cedars, spruces, pines, and junipers; or (3) tropical ones, like jade, snow rose, and olive trees. Some of us prefer to grow from the seeds because it is less expensive and because you are able to *control* the tree at every stage of its growth. That is the key word or strategy in growing bonsai trees. Bonsai trees are not cheap, like our regular annual or perennial plants, plentiful and abundantly affordable during our springtime. For bonsai lovers, it takes a lot of money to pursue this extravagant pastime.

Then we can plant a tree in a training container with the right amount of sun, water, and consistent temperature, allowing it to become sturdy and strong before we train it. Sadly, I had killed a few because of lack of knowledge, experience, proper care, and consistency for the sensitive trees. Many passed away prematurely.

Like humans, bonsai trees react to the four seasons, and knowing what happens to my bonsai tree during each season will ensure their survival and growth from winter to spring, summer, and fall. All plants, including the annuals or perennials, are sensitive to the four seasons. There are spring flowers, summer flowers, fall flowers, and a few winter decorative plants. But bonsai is for all seasons, and it requires special care for each of the four seasons of the year.

According to the instructor, fall is the best time to train a bonsai tree. And this is the critical part of raising it. I can choose one of four ways to train a tree: (1) the formal upright way, allowing it to grow naturally, with branches spreading evenly around it; (2) the informal upright way, allowing it to have a more natural slant than straight upward; (3) the slanting way, looking windblown; and (4) the more stylistic or literati way, allowing the trunk to become long and twisted with minimal branches.

So how does one train a bonsai tree? Here, meticulous, careful skills are required. It takes patience and skill for anyone to carefully *bend* the trunk and branches in the direction they want it to grow. *Control* is the key word. I visited a nursery where I saw strong wires wrapped around branches to make them conform to a certain shape or design by the grower. I thought that by using heavy-duty wires, I can *restrict or control* the potential growth of a plant, and I saw plants all becoming of different shapes that a gardener wanted for each. It is like your child; do what you want with it.

We were instructed to use three kinds of wires to *shape* the tree the way we want it to look. We must use copper wires around the trunk and branches and mold them into the shape we want. We must use finer wires on the branches and heavier ones at the bottom of the trunk. If we are not careful, the wire can bite into a tree and damage it or kill it. The goal is for the tree to grow into the shape or design we want.

With the help of a small pruning tool, we could clip off the leaves, buds, and parts of branches, always with the purpose of achieving the tree shape that we want from the beginning. This is best done during spring or autumn, when the tree has plenty of stored nutrients. According to my instructor, "Each time you prune, growth is stimulated on another part of the tree. Knowing where to prune and how often is part of the art of bonsai cultivation, and learning how to do it takes a lot of practice." And the final word of advice from the expert is, "Trimming the tree is what causes it to stay small. Otherwise, it will outgrow its container."

Lest we forget, the size of the container itself limits and restricts the growth potential of the bonsai. The smaller the pot, the smaller the tree; the bigger the pot, the bigger the tree. Control is the key to raising a prized bonsai. Everything about bonsai is control; the bonsai will grow into the shape we want.

Unfortunately, despite all the time I spent trying to learn how to raise a bonsai tree, I failed. The plant did not live to see its potential for beauty and greatness. I failed because I did not give it my full attention, patience, absolute know-how, and daily devotion to its every need, like a mother would raise her baby. But all was not in vain.

Back in the fall in China one evening, I was waiting at the main gate to the campus for a student to have dinner with me. It was a eureka moment for me because it was the first time I took notice of the two huge bonsai trees in elegant pots, one on either side of the gate. Suddenly, I saw something more than those two elegant potted trees. They reminded me of the young men and women under my care in my daily classes; their thinking, behaviors, mindsets, personal interactions, class participation, community activities, likes and dislikes, and habits were expected and predictable because of years of trimming, pruning, twisting, and shaping by their parents to be who they are today. They are the bonsai kids.

So who are these bonsai kids? In this new book, I want to focus not on China's rising economic or technological power and expansion in the world but on one important sociological fact about modern China that had affected and continues to influence the economy and the lives of millions of Chinese parents and young adults since the death of the founding father of modern communist China, Chairman Mao Zedong, in 1976. When the new leadership took over mainland China under Deng Xiaoping, the man responsible for the opening up of and radical reforms in China and exposure to the Western world, they were confronted with a mushrooming population, *tai duo ren*, meaning "too many people." The new leaders were confronted with a serious problem—how to feed the many mouths in China, still a backward and developing country at the time of Chairman Mao's death.

This book is about the bonsai kids, the children born between 1980 and 2016, the children of the one-child policy. They are the bonsai kids.

When I first arrived at the Chinese campus in September of 2008, the year of the famous Beijing Olympic Games, I was confronted with thousands of young men and women, the bonsai kids, dressed like any young people in the USA, all living inside this huge campus. Though the rich kids could afford a room in a dormitory, some stealthily also maintain an apartment outside the campus for a quiet place to pursue their studies and prepare for many exams, others to use it for their many sexual exploits. Imagine, now China has about ten million graduates from universities every year. *Tai duo ren*, too many people.

Who are these bonsai kids?

CHAPTER ONE

With the adoption and implementation in mainland China in 1980 of the one-child policy, a controversial but accepted way to curb population explosion in the post-Mao era, there emerged a new breed of *Homo sapiens* aptly labeled "little emperors," children of the modern upper-class and wealthier Chinese families who became more popular than China's beloved pandas because of the excessive amount of attention and devotion to them from their parents and grandparents. Deemed an urban phenomenon, little emperors of the one-child policy applied primarily to children of urban families.

Having the privilege as a visiting professor from the USA to work and live in China with many children of the one-child policy from both urban and rural China, I saw them more like bonsai kids— pampered, doted, and raised as if by a gardener of his cherished bonsai trees. If you understand the expensive but intricate process of producing a prized bonsai tree, you will understand my adoption of *bonsai kids*, an inclusive terminology, to describe the new generation of young men and women who are the product of the one-child policy in mainland China from 1980 to 2016.

So who are these bonsai kids? I first met them when I was a visiting American professor at a prestigious school in Fujian Province, where Pres. Xi Jinping married his second wife and spent many formative years of his life as a high-level Chinese government official. He was already tackling corruption in the government when he was in his thirties. You could go to YouTube and find a documentary on how a younger Xi Jinping tackled corruption when he was the party chief of the Communist Party of China (CPC) Ningde Prefectural Committee, 1988–1990. It states unequivocally, "A trademark of Xi Jinping is his determination to combat corruption with an iron fist, regardless of the status of the perpetrator. As early as 1990 in Ningde, Fujian Province, Xi led a successful drive to end the illegal land occupation." It marked the successful end of illegal land occupation by some top local government officials. The "tigers" and their corruption were exposed and eradicated. That was just the beginning because corruption, like cancer, continues to grow and spread throughout mainland China despite Xi's relentless efforts to root it out at every opportunity.

I also saw a video report of something he said to young government workers in Ningde, Fujian Province, something to the effect that if you want to make money, the government job is not for you. Quit and do something else. He said that because he saw that corruption is a temptation for some people to work for the government. Corruption is one way for government workers to fatten their bank accounts.

And when he ascended to power in 2013 as president of communist China, in his inaugural speech, he talked about one of the toughest challenges facing the Communist Party of China—fighting corruption. After a few months in office, he presented his "eight-point guide" or rules aimed at stricter discipline on the conduct of party officials, primarily to curb corruption and waste during official party business. And he vowed to root out "tigers and flies" or high-ranking officials and ordinary party functionaries. He vowed to combat corruption with an iron fist. He would remove the tigers and swat the flies regardless of their status in the government so he could achieve his China dream, the rejuvenation of the nation, prosperity, peace, happiness, and harmony for all. And here is the new buzzword at the moment of declaration of President Xi's ultimate goal for his government and the nation—the national goal of common prosperity or the implementation of socialism with Chinese characteristics.

I knew something about this corruption from one of my bonsai kids in the campus. Touted as the best and most secured job for life in China, many new graduates are trying to secure a government job in the midst of the current pandemic when millions are losing their jobs. But my student, when I was in China, decided not to prepare for the civil service examination (it is getting harder now with less career options and with less people passing it) to work for the government because "with President Xi Jinping, it would be difficult to make extra money working for the government." He was not ashamed of telling me that.

For years, he explained slowly to me that ordinary people would bribe government officials with a red envelope of money (*hong bao* in Chinese) or a bottle of the famous mao-tai wine if you wanted something done for you "expeditiously" unless you have some connections like a relative or a friend or a friend of a friend working in the government. In fact, one of my students, not known for his diligence in pursuit of knowledge in the campus, is now working for the Chinese government somewhere in Europe because his father knew of someone who had a friend working in the government. In mainland China, it is not what you know but who you know that will determine your fate in life. As one of my students would say to me, "Corruption is in our DNA."

For a while in China, in the news, ordinary citizens were threatening violence against or going after doctors and nurses in hospitals because ordinary citizens were tired of bribing them to do anything or more for one's parents, children, or loved ones in the hospital. Some medical professionals were injured in this violent confrontation.

One female student told me, "You have to come to my house and see all the gifts my mother had received from the parents of her students." Many of the gifts had to do with cosmetics. For some other lucky teachers, it could be a big fat *hong bao*. If you want your son or daughter to do well in school, make sure you feed the teachers with gifts or *hong bao*. Some parents are known to pay some teachers so their children could live with them and get premium attention and care, especially from those teachers in charge of critical subjects. Chinese parents all over China are known to spend enormous savings on sending their children to after-school tutorial schools or cram schools, and now the Chinese government is trying to put a stop to it so they could save some money for a new baby since most young mothers in China are complaining they could not afford a second child.

Years ago when I first came to the United States, I was reading in a popular magazine about *Japanese moms* (way before the emergence of the *tiger mother* in America), an aggressive breed of mothers who would do anything to get their little boys and girls into the best kindergartens because these institutions were connected to some of the top universities in Japan. Cram schools were very popular then in Japan. They use a different word, but cram schools are all over China. I would learn, then, that in Japan it was not the degree in college that mattered but the prestige of the university you graduated from that would determine your success because Japan would hire the top students from top universities and train them, in their own way, to work in their companies. You could say that Japan also had their distinctive Japanese bonsai kids raised by their unique Japanese bonsai moms.

CHAPTER TWO

In 2011, I was busy minding my own business, teaching as a visiting professor in mainland China, when a literary tsunami took place in the USA with the publication of a book by someone named Amy Chua about her strict parenting style in raising her two daughters the Chinese Confucianist way. *Battle Hymn of the Tiger Mother* details her iron-willed decision to raise Sophia and Lulu her way. I was totally distracted by the term *tiger mother* and decided to find this tiger in the Chinese zodiac because Amy Chua was born on the year of the tiger. Many things that the Chinese zodiac says about me are true, so I decided to find out more about this *tiger mother*. Amy Chua and I live in two different worlds, but the zodiac might give me a clue about this female author. According to the Chinese zodiac, here are the strengths of a tiger:

1. Manly, passionate, brave, with unusual spirit of adventure, love to take challenges;
2. Ambitious, energetic, optimistic, and dare to blaze new trails, think and act;
3. Trustworthy and never break promise;
4. Philanthropic, righteous, open and upright, and easy to be trusted by others;
5. Dignified and confident, born to be a leader;
6. Resolute, uncompromising, and never give up until achieve the goal.

We have never met, but I believe in my Chinese zodiac. And this brief description of a tiger gives me a window to understand the character of Amy Chua.

So who is Amy Chua? Born in America to a Chinese family who once emigrated from China to the Philippines and later to the USA, she is the John M. Duff Jr. professor of law at Yale Law School, specializing in international business transactions, law and development, ethnic conflict, and globalization and the law. Her parents were very educated people; her father was a professor of electrical engineering and computer science at the University of California, Berkeley.

Essentially, she argues that Western parents tend to focus on children's individuality, providing the environment conducive to their pursuit of their own passions, while Chinese parents, like her, believe in arming their children with whatever that are necessary or required to face life's uncertain future and journey on their way to their destination in life, essentially preparing their kids to face the present and the future with the necessary tools to achieve their goals or dreams in life. So is being a tiger mother the only way to raise a new generation of bonsai kids?

For years, I had two Siamese cats, one was A, the other B, named after my high school best friends, Adam and Benjamin. And I would play with them, talk to them, eat with them, and watch their every move, especially during winters when they would spend more time and sleep with me. They would play with their neighborhood friends during summers. I grew up in a farm in Malaya, and I grew up with pigs, dogs, cats, ducks, and chickens. I spent a lot of my village time with my cats. I would play with them when they were pregnant and was there when they had their babies. So I loved my cats.

In America, my Siamese cats were good mothers. They did not listen to the lecture of Dr. Benjamin Spock or read his famous book *Baby and Child Care*, one of the best-selling books in the USA history.

Literally, his book became the bible for many aspiring mothers. He was the first pediatrician to study psychoanalysis in an attempt to understand children's needs and family dynamics. "His ideas about childcare influenced several generations of parents to be more flexible and affectionate with their children and to treat them as individuals." Amy Chua would seem the very opposite of Dr. Spock in how to raise the best babies in the world.

Having traveled the world, I saw the English (do not call them British because they are natives of England), Chinese, blacks, Mexicans, and Native Americans raise their young according to their culture, beliefs, and traditions. Who is to decide which upbringing strategy is better or superior than the other in the world? Amy Chua wants you to think her way is *the way* to raise a promising child. Of course, her daughters had publicly claimed their mother did the right thing in raising them the way she wanted them, like a gardener of the prized bonsai tree, for the world to see.

I was too busy teaching in China to pay much attention to Amy Chua. It was like someone trying to talk to me—in one ear, out the other—like water off a duck's back.

CHAPTER THREE

So who are the bonsai kids in China? I had one unhappy experience with a young female dentist, a promising bonsai kid, working in the university hospital. Her English was excellent and fluent, and I thought she had studied abroad. To my surprise, she had never left the soil of China. During my first visit, we had a wonderful dialogue and talked like we had known each other for years. And she examined my teeth thoroughly, did some cleaning, and then wrote a note for me to go to the cashier to pay for her service. Then something happened to me or her.

What happened during my second visit troubled me enormously. All she did was to ask me to open my mouth, and she did nothing but write the note for me to pay for her service. I was curious about it and asked my Chinese colleagues in the campus to explain this rather strange behavior to me. I had to travel a long distance to see her, and she did nothing during my second visit. Her action bothered me. It was unacceptable to me. It offended me. I felt cheated. I felt the female dentist was being dishonest.

"Steve, *this is China*. This is what the dentist must do if she wants to make *extra* money for her job because the government did not pay her enough. And she would keep on writing more notes, and you would keep on paying her more money."

"I get it." *This is China!*

I had my prerogative and chose not to see her again but switched to her boss, the head of the dentistry department of the hospital, also a professor in the university. His office happened to be next to the female dentist.

And President Xi is very aware of this corruption at every level of the Chinese society though he came from a privileged background. In mainland China, he would be labeled a "princeling," a child of very influential senior communist officials. An informal but derogatory categorization, a princeling is one who benefits enormously from cronyism or nepotism. The truth is many of them, like President Xi, hold high-level political positions in the upper echelon of power in communist China. Yet during the hellish period of the Cultural Revolution (1966–1976), his father, Xi Zhongxun, a minister under Chairman Mao, was tortured by Mao's men.

If you want to make money, Xi Jinping encouraged young people not to work for the government when he was a young man himself. Most Chinese in mainland China admire and adore him, their leader, because he has lifted about eight hundred million people out of poverty through his poverty alleviation programs throughout mainland China. And he continues to visit and spend time with those in very remote places in China, areas that could only be reached by foot, and those left behind during China's rapid march to wealth and prosperity since the economic reforms by Deng Xiaoping in the early 1980s. And now under the new leadership of President Xi Jinping, China continues to march forward faster than the best speed trains in modern China, with foreign investments continuing to pour in since the pandemic because they see hope and optimism in China's economic goals and ideals, being the biggest market in the world.

A new textbook on Xi Jinping Thought on Socialism with Chinese Characteristics for a New Era will be required reading, first in Shanghai elementary, middle, and high schools in September 2021, and will be introduced to all the schools nationwide in the fall. Why

Shanghai? Because it is the most cosmopolitan city in China, and this is the modus operandi of the Chinese government to introduce something new, whether it is cultural, political, social, or economic, first in a city or one particular province and later to the rest of the country. This is China.

China continues to amaze the world from being the "manufacturer" to the world into being the biggest consumer market in the world, which is one reason why many American CEOs and businessmen went to China in the first place, along with the then availability of abundant, cheap labor, and they continue to stay in China despite former president Trump's strong urging for them to return to the USA. And because of the labor shortage and rising labor costs in mainland China now, many American companies are moving their operations not back to America but to other countries in Southeast Asia like Laos, Cambodia, Thailand, Vietnam, Philippines, Malaysia, and a few to India, the next most populous country in the world (next to mainland China), with abundant, cheap labor to boot. Without a doubt, India needs China's assistance and expertise to build and improve its infrastructure if India wants to stay competitive with the rest of the world.

Money, not politics, talks and is the driving force behind major foreign countries' decision to remain in or near China. China reminds me of a huge economic pie, and everyone who is anyone wants to have a bite of it. Once, all roads led to Rome; now all the roads are seemingly converging on mainland China, some straying to her neighbors because of cheaper, abundant labor.

Most luxury items are sold in modern China because the growing middle class has the financial means to indulge in their passion for the good life. It seemed every year I saw more and more fruit stores opening for business because, with money, they could afford eating fruits, many imported, to better their health. And Japan, their immediate neighbor, benefits from the surplus Chinese money. And many Chinese children are now spreading this wealth effortlessly around the world, owning some of the most expensive houses here and there, eating in some of the most expensive restaurants on this planet, driving some of the most elegant foreign cars money can buy, and wearing the most expensive clothes to advertise their wealth. They live and spend like their parents run a money printing press. And China, before the pandemic, sent the most students to study in the USA, a critical source of revenue for many big and small American colleges and universities.

And this is the China I was exposed to when I first arrived to teach as a visiting professor, right after the 2008 Beijing Olympics. My trip to the campus was delayed because China tried, I suspected, to prevent many Americans from attending the games (August 8, 2008) for fear of anti-China protests and marches, and China was not about to be humiliated in the presence of over five thousand international reporters from all over the world. They would love to welcome me to China after the official Olympic Games.

So I arrived at the time when all the freshmen were busy marching and executing military drills all over the campus, right before the start of actual academic classes in September of 2008. Military uniforms and drills are compulsory for all incoming new freshmen every year, like an equalizer for the fat and thin, rich and poor but most importantly to instill in all the freshmen in the university their sole purpose in coming to an academic institution, to achieve oneness in purpose and goals for the success and glory of their nation and country. Pride in one's motherland is always the main goal of all government endeavors in every campus across China.

And today the debate continues in mainland China about the necessity or validity of holding, in peacetime, such compulsory military drills and communist indoctrination and training for all incoming freshmen and high school students; top government officials want Chinese citizens, especially parents, to believe it is the best equalizer for all students from different socioeconomic backgrounds. Everyone has the same and equal opportunity to enter the most critical race in life, a college education, from start to finish in four years.

Lest we forget, there are fifty-six ethnic groups in China, the largest of these groups is the Han people, which is 91.53 percent of China's population. Most of us Chinese belong to the Han ethnic group. And China adopted the Han language as the lingua franca for the whole country. The remaining 8.47 percent is composed of fifty-five very diverse ethnic minority groups, and the central government has built different universities for them, though some minority students are chosen and sent to study in the regular universities throughout China. The apartheid or the ghetto that we know in the Western world does not exist in mainland China. It is a known fact that China continues its long-term policy to introduce the Han people into every ethnic group within the borders of mainland China. It is like socialization on a national scale. The Chinese government did this in Tibet. They also did this in Xinjiang.

This is China. And this socialization process happens in all the campuses in China at the beginning of each school year. The compulsory military training is the best equalizer for all the students from different socioeconomic backgrounds from across the length and breadth of modern China. All must share the same goal in the same campus; together, we will succeed in all our undertakings in life.

Of course, nothing is for free; and all first year college students, over eight million or so each school year, are expected to pay for everything related to the military training, though most will give their uniforms away to many needy migrant workers at the end of the training. No doubt some will see the compulsory military training as another one of the government's moneymaking ventures.

You wonder why the Chinese government is so rich. The military training is mostly paid by the students themselves. This is China. All public schools and universities are owned and run by the Chinese government. And it should not surprise anyone that the Chinee government, each year, will give scholarships to many students, rich and poor, from many countries that are friends of China, and it is the government's prerogative to send them to any Chinese university they want. This and the Belt and Road Initiative, mainly on improving the infrastructure of any country interested to work with China using Chinese expertise and financial support, are obvious but aggressive ways that China is using to spread its influence to the four corners of this planet. From President Xi's predecessor to the current president, China openly denies any interest to "colonize" the world.

This is China. So will this massive, comprehensive, and intensive nationwide peacetime military training or a simple introduction to rigorous academic pursuits by all incoming freshmen prepare students for participation in a new war? I seriously doubt they will have the requisite physical stamina or willpower to fight in a war. Many are labeled spoiled children, the products of the one-child policy since the early '80s.

These are the bonsai kids. They have been raised, according to China watchers and critics of China's one-child policy, as parasites by overindulging and doting parents and grandparents, not as war machines to fight in a war. Many students do not think the late summer heat was the best time for the training; a few schools will decide to hold it at a later date when the weather is not as hot.

And as a foreign teacher, my presence is not required. As a Chinese myself, I understand the rationality behind the government's policy to require all incoming freshmen to undergo these physically draining exercises, a foundation required for a successful four-year academic regiment. All freshmen will remember some key concepts from the training: equality, discipline, focus, teamwork, and harmony. At the end of the military training, many will discover their strengths and weaknesses and their common purpose in pursuing a college education, preparing them to be responsible citizens of one unified country. And hopefully, many will find the answer to the most pressing question in their lives: What does it mean to be a Chinese in a country of about 1.4 billion inhabitants?

No matter what the future has in store for them, one thing is for sure: together, they will succeed and conquer the world. Collectivism, not American-style individualism, reigns supreme in China. They are simply following President Xi Jinping's China dream. It is a collective dream that together, no matter who they are, they will all work in solidarity to improve their country's well-being, life, happiness, harmony, and prosperity. It is socialism with Chinese characteristics, the Chinese way. This is China.

CHAPTER FOUR

It might just surprise the Chinese government how much some of these bonsai kids hated to attend public lectures related to dear Lenin, Marx, Mao, or communism. They were told their presence or attendance at these public lectures was required, or else they would face some sort of punishment related to their academic grades (unheard of in any academic institution in the USA). "There will be someone there at the entrance to the lecture hall to check your attendance," students would say angrily to me.

Resigned to fate because they had no choice but to attend these public lectures as part of their continued indoctrination of Mao's communist thinking, they told me, "We had listened to this bullshit about Lenin, Marx, and Mao since primary school. We are tired of it." They moaned and groaned about it. I thought then they were being ungrateful bonsai kids.

They expressed their opposition verbally. *Typical youth of modern China,* I thought. To many of my students, America means freedom, not China. And as long as they live in China, they feel trapped and suffocated by the culture and traditions that will define who they are as Chinese.

From the start of my college teaching in China, I was wrong to assume that most students would welcome the many opportunities with open arms, hearts, and souls to listen to veteran communists about their past growing up and living in communist China. And now as young adults, they are tired of the whole bullshit (in their language). The sponges could not absorb anymore. *Too much of a good thing is not good for your mental health*, they seemed to be telling me. I sensed the frustration and total indifference to more communist education. I could only empathize with their genuine frustrations and lack of individual freedom.

What was most troubling to me is the fact that many top students, invited to join the Communist Party on campus, refused outright to become a member. Only the best and the brightest students are invited to join the Communist Party. For a while, it is true that "party membership symbolizes status, power, opportunity and sometimes privilege; therefore, it is extremely difficult to be accepted by the Party and to become a formal member."

Without a doubt, the college students are very troubled by the corruption among the party members, and they do not want to be a part of that system. (They saw what happened to Bo Xilai, now in prison for serious corruption, someone who could have taken the place of President Xi.) Students told me their parents would urge them to join the Communist Party. Granted, it was true years ago that if you were a member of the Communist Party, you would be assigned prestigious jobs after college graduation. The communist government had now stopped this practice.

During my seven years on the campus, students would ask me for my advice about joining the Communist Party. "As long as you live in China, my advice to you is simple: join the party. We cannot predict the future. If anything, membership in the Communist Party means your love for your country and also your loyalty to China." I would often say this to students who came to me for advice. Somehow many of them trusted my judgment and advice on issues related to their studies, love, sex, parents, careers, and future. But a few of the students ignored the invitation to join the party. They would ignore their parents' concern for their future and membership in the Communist Party.

Some bonsai kids have a mind of their own. The future of any nation is its young people. Should I be concerned?

CHAPTER FIVE

It was an honor to be teaching the bonsai kids of today in modern China. I was impressed with the student body and the huge campus because almost all students would travel to distant cities to attend colleges as far away as possible from their hometowns, many in remote parts of mainland China. There are no universities in small towns in mainland China.

My campus is so big that many students will ride their bicycles to attend the different classes in buildings scattered across the campus. Later, some campuses would use certain vehicles to take students to different buildings in a vast campus, while most would enjoy cycling or walking to their destinations daily.

It slowly dawned on me that all was not well in the campus, especially among the male students. Some female students would confess to me that they, too, had their own problems in their dormitories. Many grew up without brothers or sisters, and so they were very individualistic and isolated when they came to the campus. They did not grow up interacting with other kids in a family because they were the only child. (In America, it is not uncommon for children to spend weekends with friends, playing and doing fun things together. They eat together. They play together. They sleep together. Most American children do that.) Some were inconsiderate to others in the same room, usually four students to a room. Some universities had introduced, for those who could afford it, one or two students to a room.

One student came to me and told me he had no choice but to move out to live outside the campus because he could not tolerate the selfishness of some of his roommates. "My three roommates hate me. They would travel together to the city on weekends without me. They would share some snacks in the room, deliberately leaving me out. They might even cook something, and I was not invited to eat with them. They would watch the American basketball games together with some Chinese beer. They would make life miserable for me to live with them." I told him to talk to the campus counselor.

Sadly, my campus did not have a full-time counselor who had a degree in psychology or counseling, and a troubled student would have no choice but to move out of the dormitory to another. If they had the money, a few would move out of the campus and live by themselves, though illegal by the college rules. I met one such student, and he approached a counselor, a professor in the campus. And he was told to return to his dormitory room and discuss the problem with his roommates. I told him to see the counselor because he and his roommates did not have the skills to deal with the problem.

One university somewhere in the south was experimenting with something new in China. This university came up with an idea to put a retired old professor in some dormitories. The purpose was to help students with their studies and relationships with one another. It would be great if the Ministry of Education in China would implement this throughout the country because children of one-child families were labeled selfish and uncaring and not used to living with other young people in their lives. If these bonsai kids could not study and work harmoniously with other students in the campus, how could we expect them to function in the real world where they have to work with people from different cultural or socioeconomic backgrounds in China? The campus is a microcosm of the real world outside.

In my classes, I did not encounter any tension or conflict among my students as they sat happily together to listen to me. But if you were to visit the campus in the late afternoons or evenings, you would be surprised to see many students studying by themselves in different buildings across the campus (unheard of in America). Since they could not study in their own rooms, most students would study in different classrooms daily. This was true in my campus. That was something very unusual to me because most American students would love to study with their friends.

I was told by a few students about this odd behavior in China. Most students preferred to study by themselves because they were thinking, *What if my friend got an A and I got a C in a test? Why should I be bothered to study with my friends? Why bother to share my knowledge?* Lack of trust in others was a major reason why most students chose to study by themselves, unless they had boyfriends or girlfriends.

I did my best to encourage them to study and work together because, in the real business world, teamwork is the key to success. It must begin in our campus in China. Some professors would introduce teamwork in their classroom teaching. Still, I had students telling me that not all students would work harmoniously together to achieve a common goal. Instead, some members of a team would not participate fully in the team assignment, while one or two might carry the burden for all.

What about teamwork among the professors in the campus? I was teaching in a big campus; for us teachers, there were free bicycles we could use to travel from one building to another, requiring us to sign in each time and return the keys after use. There were a few irresponsible, unscrupulous, or selfish professors who kept the keys while the bicycles were parked outside a building. Because of this, there were times we could not find the keys to the bicycles around the campus. What happened to the team spirit among the professors? As a foreigner and a guest of the institution, I was told not to rock the boat; I just learned to accept it. "This is China," I was told. At the time, it was a bitter pill to swallow.

I thought I was smart, so I bought my own bicycle, but it was stolen after a week despite the guards' presence at the campus gates. I got smart the second time because I decided to buy an old bicycle that was not of much value to a would-be thief. I had the same old bicycle during the years I was teaching in the campus.

There were bicycles everywhere in the campus. And there would be at least one bicycle shop inside, selling you new and used bicycles or repairing your bike. I would not be surprised if some of the bicycles belonged to students who had graduated from the university and were left there unclaimed by anyone.

During my years of teaching in the university, I had not seen any student owning a scooter, a motorcycle, or a car. One or two students might have an electric bicycle. They were few. One reason was obvious: public transportation was easy, accessible, and cheap, whether by taxi or bus or boat. And speed trains could take you from city to city easily and quickly in any part of China. And there were drivers who would pick you up at your doorstep from town to town. That was simple and cheap.

CHAPTER SIX

At first, I taught freshman journalism at a prestigious university; and for the next six years, I would be teaching American culture and history, world events, and British culture and history at a private college located in the same campus. I liked world events the most because it was open to any student from any department in the campus who was interested in improving their English while having the opportunity to learn the major events happening around the world. The other two classes were strictly for students majoring in English in the English Language Department.

Thinking back about my assignment, I still feel bad and guilty that my boss gave me the classes of a Chinese female teacher who had been teaching these courses for a number of years. Since I am an American and have a sister living in the United Kingdom, my boss must have assumed I would be a better or a more qualified person to teach the courses. That is my conjecture. But I feel guilty of robbing the Chinese lady of her job.

From the start, I adhered religiously to the curriculum. It was not my choice but expected of me. That meant teaching, if possible, every word from the book. I called that spoon-feeding the kids. That is the style of teaching in China, all the way from elementary to junior to high school and now to college. And soon I would discover that the best students were those who could regurgitate every word they had been taught in the class. The A students were those who could literally produce the answers verbatim from the textbooks. Memorization or rote learning is the key to success in Chinese schools and colleges. And this is undoubtedly the biggest challenge facing all Chinese students who plan to study in the West, whether in the UK, the USA, Australia, or Canada, where we teach our students to be proactive, creative thinkers, and independent researchers and to have more free time to explore the world. It is like living in a different world.

A bonsai kid once told me that a professor had given him a lower grade because he was not able to use the exact words from the textbook. He was given a lower grade for trying to express his understanding and interpretation of the question and his own wording of the answer. *How sad is that?* I thought at the time. *What is teaching? What is learning in China?* For this reason, many younger Chinese parents are sending their children abroad, especially to America because of the American style of teaching, allowing students more room for initiative and creative thinking.

Having traveled to many countries around the world, usually to visit friends or relatives, I had many resources to make my classroom presentation interesting and more palatable to my students, who were always hungry for anything from outside China. Many of my students had written in their essays the one dream in their lives: "I am learning English now so, one day, I can use it to get to know the world. I want to travel around the world." Bonsai kids, children of the one-child policy, are most receptive to the Western ways of thinking, new thoughts, and new ideas. They participate in or celebrate all the major Western festivals in China. And now the Chinese government is trying to stop all Western ideas from entering the classes in China. Now they are trying to ban certain Western books. Banning foreign teachers could be next.

For my first Christmas in China, my students gave me an apple. Why a preciously wrapped apple for Christmas? The Chinese word for *apple* is *ping guo*. My students told me that the tradition of giving apples on Christmas Eve came from the similarity of the Chinese word for *apple* (*ping guo*) to the Chinese word for *Christmas Eve* (*ping'an ye*). In Chinese, *ping* means "peace." Christmas is about peace on earth.

And of course, many Chinese students also love Western movies and American basketball, including adopting Western words or names for their English names. One of my students called himself Anonymous, and he was proud to tell the whole class that he got it from the renowned *Oxford Dictionary*. Never mind that he did not know the meaning of the word. When I asked him, "Why use this word as your name?"

"I like the sound of it," he said confidently in class.

So I received many individually wrapped apples from my students, their way of showing me they loved and respected me. In return, I could be the first foreign teacher to show them how to make chocolate sauce (melting the chocolate bars with milk) on which to dip their apple chunks. That was also my first time making chocolate sauce, though I had known about it for years living in the USA. The bonsai kids are always hungry for things and ideas that are American, not just Western.

An early survey, according to my students, revealed that no one slept in my classes while I was teaching. What an honor to be told that by my students. The dean who hired me invited me to her office one day to tell me that the students in the English Language Department had voted me as the second most popular teacher. She made it clear that it should be a great honor because I was the first foreign teacher to receive such a distinction. And who was the most popular teacher according to this survey? The dean herself, of course.

Of course, I took advantage of being a well-respected foreign teacher in the campus. I demanded what I wanted, like two air conditioners in my apartment instead of one, and that I would not teach 8:00 a.m.

classes. I was evil and corrupt to the marrow of my bones. Or was it "Strike while the iron is hot"?

So how did I achieve this honor of being the most respected foreign professor in the campus? I did not read books on how to become a popular professor or teacher to my students. Many of the things I did came naturally to me. In fact, a student did ask me how to be popular in the campus. By then, I had my talk show, and many students had come to know me. I did not come to teach in China to become popular. I came here to teach. Most importantly, I came here with many ideas on how best to assist my students to achieve their potential, dreams, and goals in life. I told the inquisitive student, "Think of what you can do for the community of students. That would be a good start on your journey to becoming popular in the campus." This same student would later reject an offer to pursue a PhD because "it is time to make some money for myself."

On the very first day, I made it clear to my students that, in the United States, the best students are the ones who will sit closest to the professor in the front rows of the classroom. I said this because those students who wanted to play with their phones preferred to sit way back in the classroom so they could pursue their own agenda. Not in my classes. I deliberately filled the wastepaper basket with paper one day because I was about to tell my students what would happen to their phone if I found them looking at it or using it while I was trying to educate them. I dropped it carefully into the basket—a simple lesson about what would happen to their phone if they were caught playing with it. You see, I believe a word to the wise is sufficient.

For those still not convinced of moving to the front rows in the classroom, I had good news for them. I was not the type to sit on a comfortable chair and teach to the class or read from my notes at a podium; it was my habit to walk around the classroom at all times. And I would be standing an inch away from you if I suspected you were up to no good, if you continued to talk to your classmate when

I was teaching, if I felt you were about to enter dreamland, or if I sensed you were about to play with your phone in class. Like a hawk, I was hovering over them in all my classes when I was teaching. With the use of the PowerPoint presentation in class, you do not need to be in front of the room at all times. I did not read from any notes like many Chinese professors, where they were stuck to the podium in front of the classroom. I had freedom to move to any part of the room at any time during my time with my bonsai kids.

Most Chinese teachers had the tendency to scold the students for whatever they did in class, humiliating them in front of their classmates as a kind of deterrent. Many Chinese parents did that too to their children. I was a different kind of teacher, and the students suspected and knew that from the first day they entered my classroom.

My American approach to all my bonsai kids is that there is a time for everything. When you come to the classroom, it is time to learn and learn and learn. I made a mistake one day when I heard a phone ringing, and without a second thought, I told the student to leave the class so he could respond to it. What a mistake! He was away for a long time. It would never happen again in my class. When he did finally return to the class, I had this important message for all my students: Tell your parents or boyfriend or girlfriend that you have plenty of time to talk to them after class. Pay full attention when you are in my class. Tell them to call you when you are not in class. There is a time for everything, unless it is an emergency call, like a call from the president of China in Beijing.

CHAPTER SEVEN

I met a female professor at an airport one time, and we were able to share our experiences in teaching this new breed of students in China, children of the one-child policy. She also had a high administrative position in the university where she was teaching. She shared an interesting experience of a female student who came to her for a letter of recommendation. "When the student told me she was my student, I told her I do not remember seeing her in my class. But she wanted me to write her a letter of recommendation. I could not do it because I do not recognize her at all. Sad but true."

That was why I told my students on the first day of class, "One day you might ask me to write you a letter of recommendation. Sit in the front rows so I can see you and recognize you. But that is not enough. You must also actively participate in the classroom. I want to see your active classroom participation. I want to hear your voice. I want to know what you know. And I want to hear your voices, your ideas, your opinions, your thinking. You must do all that and more if you want your professor to write you a strong letter of recommendation at the end of your college career."

Soon I would learn from a few students that the reason for staying silent or quiet in class and not actively participating in any kind of discussion or the sharing of their ideas was that they did not want their friends or classmates to think they were trying to show off their knowledge or impress others with their brilliance or intelligence.

Modesty, I would soon learn, is a prized virtue in China. Shockingly to me as an American, they told me it would be disrespectful to ask teachers questions or express an opinion while a teacher was teaching.

But I did not want what happened to that female student to happen in my classes. Students have been writing their own letters of recommendation as I was told by many of my students. And a professor will just sign it. I hope most Western institutions of higher education, desperate for Chinese money from Chinese students, get wind of this and question the authenticity of most of these letters of recommendation coming from mainland China.

I did write a few letters of recommendation during my seven years as a visiting professor based on my intimate knowledge of them inside and outside the classrooms, especially their ardent pursuits in extracurricular activities helping the community or other students to have a better education. Like most American universities, I want to know what they do when they are not studying.

CHAPTER EIGHT

The dean of my school appreciated what I did for her students and many from other departments in the campus. At first, she was not happy that I had spent time with other students, and she called me to her office to talk about it. I told her the truth: students came looking for me. For this reason, after the first few weeks, I stopped eating in the student canteen because there would always be students who took the opportunity to talk to me or to sit with me at the table. At times, I wanted to be left alone to enjoy my meals or to spend my precious time with a particular student.

The dean and I worked together to implement our goals for students in our English Language Department with focus on listening, speaking, reading, and writing, the four critical aspects for anyone who wants to master the English language. As a college professor, I knew from my own experiences growing up as a Chinese that I must learn to listen well if I want to speak well. And I must learn to read well if I want to write well. Basically, I learned the basic concepts of input and output when the internet first started in the USA.

Together, she and I introduced the first school-wide Speak English Bracelet project because, within the first months, I would soon discover many students across the campus were shy or afraid to speak English to another student. So I came up with this Speak English Bracelet as a way for students to conquer their fears or lack of confidence when trying to speak English to someone in campus.

I had very little patience with students who told me they would not speak English because "we are all Chinese in the campus." Wearing this simple bracelet would give you the confidence to speak English to anyone who was also wearing it, a simple idea. I would later introduce this concept to another university in the province.

The dean and I also launched this Speak English Bracelet with our first talk show, hosted by me, in our campus, aiming "to expose all our Chinese students to foreign voices, and also voices of students who are fluent in English, and to give them the opportunity to express their thoughts, ideas and thinking in the audience, and for them to ask questions of the guest or the host, all in English." It was something very new in the campus, with the sole purpose of allowing all students a chance to use, practice, and improve their English language since they had been introduced to it since they were in the third grade in elementary school.

Korean, Japanese, and Chinese students all suffer from the same disease: they learn the English language at an early age, but there is no urgency to speak the language. I found it in Japan, and they disdain outsiders who do not try to speak Japanese, their language. I am not sure about Korea. In China, students learn English because they want to study abroad. The ability to speak English is never their top priority, but writing is.

The dean and I also believed we should provide all our students opportunities to learn from and interact with foreign guests in our Western Culture Month. And each year, students from all departments would work freely and diligently in campus-wide competitions in drama, debate, dubbing, writing, and public speaking, all in the endeavor to improve their English language proficiency. She and I worked hard to urge the college to open an English center to provide an environment that is conducive to the learning and mastery of the English language, a place where only English is the preferred currency.

One of my students in the English department and I worked together for him to participate in the local, regional, and national speech contests. He went all the way to Beijing, the capital of China, for the nationals. We met when he was a first year student, raised by a mother, without a father. And I promised him if he did well in his studies, I would one day send him to study in the United States. From that day on, he would receive scholarship money every semester during his four years in college. This was something new to me. In the school, at the end of each semester, each department would post the names of the top students, and each would receive some scholarship money (unheard of in the USA). I promised to send him to study in the USA. He understood what I said, but more importantly, he knew what he must do to achieve his goal.

I did something else for him. When he told me his roommates had this or that and he was envious of their privileged background, I also gave him what he wanted, a good mountain bike because he wanted to use it to go home to visit his mother. And I sent him to visit some cities during the holidays. Yes, I sent him with a group of university students in China to visit America during one national holiday. After his return to China, he could not wait for the day he could go back to study in the USA.

His roommates must be wondering where he got the money to pursue his dreams, a secret strictly between the two of us. I kept my promise, and eventually, I sent him to study in the United States of America for a master's degree. Today he is teaching in an international school—a school for the rich who can afford the high tuition, especially for those interested in preparing to study abroad.

I also kept my promise to a freshman in my first journalism class. I was so impressed with a story he wrote that I promised him that, one day, I would publish it as a children's book. Eventually, I did publish it. He is finishing his PhD in journalism and will teach in a college in China.

CHAPTER NINE

After the dean told me she did not want me to establish a scholarship in my name, I decided to help students who had shown great potential in their academic and career pursuits. I did this because it became obvious to me that not all students came from well-to-do families. Not many were little emperors and princesses. In fact, many borrowed money from the banks with low interest rates because all the banks in China are owned and operated by the Chinese government.

After eating a few meals with my students in the college canteen, it became obvious to me that the Chinese government subsidized all the foods served in the different canteens in our campus. Those students from wealthy families chose to eat in many restaurants outside the campus. Not all bonsai kids were from well-to-do families.

I saw this one shortsighted student in the campus. He was not my student. But I decided to do something with his poor eyesight. I took him to an optical shop outside the campus and gave him a pair of glasses. I would remember forever what he wrote to me in a short email: "Thank you, Steve. Now I could see much better the PowerPoint in my classes." It was just a small gift from me, but it made a huge difference in his life. I know you don't have to be rich like Jack Ma in China or Bill Gates in the USA to offer some kindness or generosity to many who are less privileged than many of us.

During my first year in the campus, I saw this young man hopping with a wooden crutch that his father had made for him to use ever since he was old and strong enough to use it. He told me a car ran over his leg when he was a child. He was not my student, but I could not help watching him almost daily from a distance. He was a handsome tall young man with dark skin. And he was strong and muscular. And he would hop very fast from place to place in the campus on his crutch. And so I arranged to meet him. I found one of my students who could translate for me since I did not speak Chinese. This crippled student was majoring in mechanical engineering, not English.

I arranged to meet him in the lobby of the college hotel. Most universities in China operate their own hotels inside the huge campus for visitors, parents, teachers, or visiting scholars or professors. We found a quiet place in this huge lobby in our college hotel. Little did I know that he could speak English very fluently with me. That was the first surprise.

"I want you to know that there are many handicapped or disabled people in modern China, and I am not sure you will get the help you need to walk again from your government. I would like to help you walk again. What do you think?" I said this because of what I saw when I was walking in front of a store one day on a very busy weekend. And there were people everywhere, young and old. Sitting on the pavement in front of a store was a very handicapped young man. He moved me to tears because he could not walk but sat there and begged for help, and nobody seemed to pay attention to him. I thought, *The government should do something for him so he would not have to beg for help from the indifferent, cold-blooded public.*

However, I also witnessed something incredible at one public event. In the big crowd, I saw an adult in his wheelchair. He was able to navigate his wheelchair in the crowd, selling small souvenirs to strangers. What a way to make a living! I was inspired that this young adult had a will to live and to make something of his life despite having to use his wheelchair because of his deformed body.

The truth is many Chinese avoid him because, in some strange way, they believe your deformity is a sign of bad luck as if punished by some divine being from the heavens. That is why, in China, many parents will gladly throw away or abandon such children. Most people will avoid you.

Things are not good in China to the extent that the Chinese government was tempted to pass a "good Samaritan law" to encourage ordinary citizens to help those in need, wherever it might be. There was a terrible accident of a young girl knocked over by a car and left to die on the road, and people simply walked by as if nothing had happened. It was in the news for days across China.

There was a big debate whether the central government could legislate how you should love your parents. Many were now left in rural areas, and their young adult children had simply disappeared from their lives. That was why I felt I must do something for this young student with one leg, using a wooden crutch made by his father.

He was an educated young man, and I was not about to beat around the bush. I was being honest with him, and I wanted to help him. He kept silent for a while and wasn't sure what to make of what I had said to him. A foreigner? Nobody in his country had ever offered him any kind of help.

And here was the second surprise. He actually said no to my kind gesture. I was new to China, and I would learn from other students the reason for this young man's reluctance to accept my kind offer. "You know, Steve," another student told me frankly about the matter, "the reason why this young man was reluctant to accept your offer is simple, that is, if you know anything about our Chinese culture. To accept your offer of kindness or generosity means he will be indebted to you for now and the rest of his life."

"I am not aware of that."

"Maybe he does not want to be obligated to you for the rest of his life. And for that reason, he finds it difficult to accept your generosity. Does it make sense to you?" I never thought about it that way.

I met the young man again, and we continued our conversation about his inability to walk but more about my concern for his future and career. It would be great if he could walk again.

Now here was the third surprise. Friends, cousin brothers, and some students told me he was very good at playing basketball in the campus with just one leg. His cousin brother told me that, when they were teenagers, his father took them to climb a mountain somewhere in China. "My father was surprised that he could climb up the mountain quicker and faster than me. And I have two legs. I was exhausted using my hands and legs to climb up a mountain. But my cousin brother had no problem doing it with just one leg."

And when we talked again, I wanted to make sure he fully understood my motive for wanting him to walk again. "This would be my *gift* to you. I want you to walk again. You are not obligated to pay me back." I made sure he fully understood the meaning of the word *gift*, something freely given with no strings attached. For the first time, he broke into a smile. I was encouraged.

Now the fourth surprise—the Chinese New Year was around the corner, and that meant all students would be leaving for home for about a month of vacation. The campus would be empty. He wanted to know if he could have the prosthetic leg now. Now? "This is a holiday, and you would have to return home to your parents. There would not be anyone here in the campus. Maybe we can plan to have you examined by an orthopedic surgeon first after you returned from the vacation."

I made the decision to fly home with him since I would be out of school for the same one-month duration. I did this because I really wanted to know more about his family and his background. Both parents were migrant workers. He had a brother and a sister, taking care of themselves in a very small house in a small farm (somewhere near the famous city of Chongqing) with no room for a guest like me. I was to stay with his uncle, a famous local high school math teacher. And he had two cousin brothers also in colleges away from home.

His father was the oldest in the family, and in the old days, that meant you worked to support the rest of the family. And you did not have the opportunity to go to school. And that would happen often to girls in the family. The second boy was the math teacher.

The third or the youngest boy had a good college degree, now working for the government. And he drove me around in his expensive American car. And that meant he had money, but the youngest uncle did nothing for the boy with one leg. I was not happy when I found this out because I, as a visiting professor from America, was trying to give him a prosthetic leg so he could have a better future, while his rich uncle did not even bother to give him a modern crutch.

He never knew how upset I was about his uncle doing nothing for him. Instead, he was hopping around with a wooden crutch (without any padding on it) that his own father made for him to use all his young life. He was eager to be fitted with a prosthetic leg, and so we flew back to the campus. There was no one in there.

We were very lucky. I took him to the best hospital in the city and found an orthopedic surgeon who happened to be trained in the United States of America. I was surprised and encouraged by his kindness and generosity to the student and me.

"You are an American, and you are doing this for a Chinese student in your campus. The least I could do is to offer him my service. It would be my gift to him." That was the fifth surprise. He examined the student and told us no surgery would be required for him to have a prosthetic leg. Though his leg was amputated above the knee, he was sure we should not encounter any major problem for a prosthetic leg.

I took a picture of him with one leg and sent it to two friends, both practicing doctors in Melbourne, Australia. These were friends of mine from Malaysia, where I came from. One friend said to me, "Steve, go ahead with the prosthetic leg. I know why you want to do this. It's because you grew up very poor yourself, and you want to do something for this young man in China. Go ahead. I will help you." Both of my doctor friends sent me money so the three of us could finance the new prosthetic leg for the student.

We had plenty of time before returning to classes for the student to start walking again with a new prosthetic leg. Now the only problem was he cannot play basketball anymore. What an irony!

And now the final surprise. I found through his cousin that he was depressed for days because of something happening in his campus. When the university found out about this young man with a prosthetic leg, they wanted to make a video about him to share the story with a wider audience. A national student magazine did a story of us together, focusing more on a father's love for his son because of the wooden crutch that his father had made for him throughout his life. The local newspaper and TV also did a story about him. And many students expressed surprise and gratitude to me personally for what I did for him.

And I had said via the mass media to all the students in the campus, "I know you are busy with your books. Many of you have expressed to me, 'I wish I had done something for this student, but I was too busy with my books.' When you see someone in need, do something, however small your contribution. The world is waiting for you, for your kindness and generosity. Do it now because that opportunity might not come again."

The student with the prosthetic leg was depressed because he did not want to appear in a video by the university. Finally, I was able to squeeze the truth out of him. "Steve, I just want to be left alone. I just want to pursue my education. I do not want to be a role model to other students. I do not want that responsibility on my shoulders." I understood every word he said, and I told the university about it.

Today he has a PhD in mechanical engineering, now teaching in a prestigious university in China. I wish for a fairy-tale ending to every student I encountered when I was a visiting professor in China.

Every day a new adventure was hiding in the bush, so to speak. And I continued to learn more about this whole new breed of young people, the children of the one-child policy since its inception at the beginning of the '80s. Every encounter was a new adventure for me. Who are the bonsai kids?

CHAPTER TEN

I was introduced to a female graduate student as she was preparing for an interview with an important institution for a notable job. We never met personally, but everything was done through the computer. We were able to discuss many major issues confronting the women in modern China. What is the role of women in modern China and the Chinese society? Why is it important to include women in our government today? Chairman Mao himself, the founding father of modern China, was quoted to have said, "Women can hold up half the sky," which was instrumental in advancing the protection of women's legal rights across China.

Two heads are better than one, and so we tried to cover every aspect of the importance of women in modern China. I was preparing her for a critical interview for an important job. She was confident she was prepared for the interview.

Then one day she called me on the phone to thank me for our thorough preparation, and she told me what happened at the interview. "Here is the surprise for you. They only asked me one question, a simple one. 'Tell me something about yourself.'"

What? I could not believe my ears. Tell me something about yourself? Is that all? I was indeed taken by surprise because we had talked, discussed, and reviewed every possible question for her interview.

My assumption was that they did not ask her questions to test her knowledge. She was an outstanding graduate student. They simply wanted to know if she could communicate fluently in English.

Almost the same thing happened to another female student. This time, she wanted to do well in the oral or spoken portion of a test that would allow her to study in a foreign university. Someone asked me if I would be willing to assist her to pass this exam. We met in the lobby of the same hotel in the campus.

"So you did not do well in the spoken part of your test. You got a very low mark in spoken English. Any idea why?" I asked, hoping she would offer a clue about why she had failed the test three times already. Granted, she was a shy girl, but we were talking about taking and passing a test to help her study abroad.

I got a little impatient for once, and finally, I asked her a simple question. "Can you tell me something about your mother?" All I wanted was to hear her say something, anything. But she could not or would not say anything about her mother.

Finally, I started talking. "My mother? My mother is an incredible woman, a very independent woman. But she is a very kindhearted woman. She would help anyone in need in our neighborhood and in my school."

"Not true. I cannot say that." She broke the silence.

"I don't care if it is true or not. The examiner does not know you or your mother. You must say something if you want to pass the oral test. I see your problem."

She simply stared at me like I was a lunatic of sorts. "Say something. It does not matter if it is true or not. You must open your mouth if you want to pass the next oral test," I told her. She was a real disappointment to me.

Chapter Eleven

There was a young man who also disappointed me personally for very different reasons. A student in the campus told me about someone he knew in his hometown, way in the north of China. For whatever reasons, I kept ignoring him and did nothing to help his friend. Finally, I found time to know more about his poor friend in north China. And when, finally, I decided to see this poor young man from the north, I got my wish.

One day I heard the knock on my apartment door. I was informed the young man would be traveling from the north to see me in person. He had just taken the famous, dreaded Gaokao, the critical college entrance examination required of every student if they want to study in a college.

And there at the door was a young man dressed like a typical college student but with a difference. He did not have a backpack or a fancy luggage. Instead, he carried two plastic bags, like the ones used in a grocery store, one on either hand with his personal belongings. I could not believe my eyes. That poor!

He spent a week with me for us to get to know each other. He had a twin brother, but his mother ran off with the family money when they were about eleven years old. His father was a sick man and was unable to work and support the family. Both boys were raised by their grandparents after the mother disappeared. They both got lucky

41

because a teacher in their high school took care of them and helped them through high school.

In China, free education covered elementary and junior high school at the time. You need money to attended any high school. (More recently, the Chinese government was thinking about extending free education to the high schools throughout China because many students dropped out after junior high school for different reasons; one had to do with financial support.) He got lucky and was able to finish his high school, now waiting for the results of his Gaokao, which would determine his future and fate.

After we talked, I promised him I would be happy to support him to go to college if he would work hard. His Gaokao result was excellent, and he was able to enter a good university in the north of China. I was generous to him and bought him a computer for use in college. He sent me his academic report, which I had asked for because I wanted to know how well he was doing in college. I was not too happy with some low grades, but he had plenty of time to catch up.

Then he stopped sending me the so-called report card the second year. I called him and asked him to explain. I had heard from his roommate that he was doing a lot of partying here and there and was not diligent in his studies. "Why should I send you my report card? You are not my father," he said, a little impatient with me.

"What?"

"You are not my father. I will not send you the report card."

"We agreed when you came to see me that you would let me know of your studies. I do want to know how well you are doing because I am helping you financially. I have the right to know. Think again about what you just said to me."

We were going nowhere with our conversation, and I ended it abruptly. That was the end of our relationship. I had no reason to support his college education. What a disappointment.

Maybe, just maybe, if I had the patience of a saint that day, I could have directed him to leave the university and learn a skill at a vocational school in China. Something I found in China was that no parent would entertain the idea of his son or daughter attending a vocational school. In their thinking, that was for low-class people in society. That was for the students who had "no brains." "Not my son. Not my daughter. I would never allow him or her to attend a vocational school, not in China." Instead, I made the decision to end our friendship and relationship.

I told my students a time or two in my classes that not all of them were "college material," that it might be better for some to pursue a vocational education at a reliable school. At the time, I did encourage the brother of one of my students to attend a vocational school. He rejected my financial assistance because "many vocational schools are not doing much to help us learn a skill or prepare us for a career. It is a waste of money and my time. I would not go near one." I sadly accepted his rejection of my generosity. At the time, I did talk to many of my students, and they seemed to confirm the truth about vocational schools in China. It was a waste of money to attend one.

But one day a newspaper headline got my attention and got me very interested to read the story. "Student who dropped out of Peking University has 'no regrets.'" Peking University is one of the top schools in mainland China, like Harvard or Yale in the USA. And it went on to say, "A student is learning basic lathe and doing work at Beijing Polytechnic, the biggest vocational school in the Chinese capital." The student was learning some technical skills.

The story was about a student who decided that he must drop out of Peking University to study in a vocational or technical school. He was one of the "top local scorers" of Gaokao in Qinghai Province, and so he planned originally to attend Beijing Institute of Aeronautics. He had no choice but to follow his father's wish for him to enter Peking University to study life sciences. Too much focus on the theory of life sciences troubled him, and in his third year, he left the university to study numerical control at Beijing Industrial Technical College, one of the technical schools in Beijing.

He said this about his decision to drop out of Peking University: "I was very fortunate to make the choice six years ago. What I'm learning now is also very helpful to people's life. I believe everyone can become powerful if they find what best fits their interest and needs." He knew Peking University was not for him. And against his father's desire, he made an important decision to follow his own dream, to study at a technical school so he could learn a skill that would benefit humanity.

It is common knowledge in China that very few bonsai kids will dare to do anything against their parents' decision. Most will follow what their parents want, like chickens following the trail of food on the ground. That is why I call them bonsai kids, the by-product of years of taking care and raising a bonsai tree in the way you want it to be or look like, following your every whim and fancy and design. So what this one student did, leaving Peking University, was very unusual, going against the wish of his father. He had no regrets leaving the halls of Peking University. He was one of the best students at the technical college. And even before his graduation, "many companies have already made him job offers."

One response I came across from a student gives us hope for the future: "Vocational schools are as essential as universities in terms of their role in society, and there is no shame in studies and careers." The real challenge is how to convince the many college students and their parents of this truth, that at the moment China needs more graduates from vocational schools, not colleges and universities, with focus on acquisition of practical skills that are in high demand in modern China.

Americans went to Germany to study why many German students would rather enter vocational schools than regular universities. And those who graduated from vocational schools in Germany would end up pursuing careers that are beneficial to society. These students are well respected in today's German society, not so in America or China because many Americans, like the Chinese, do not entertain the idea that some of their daughters and sons might be better off if they pursue skills in vocational schools and not paper degrees from colleges.

Anyway, in June 2014, China unveiled a long-term plan to support vocational education in the country, especially in "talents training system." We must not forget the story of the millions of migrant workers coming from the rural areas who have helped build the modern cities and skyscrapers across China and the millions who continue to help keep the machines and engines of factories running in the last four decades or so. And these millions have radically changed the social, cultural, economic, and political landscapes of China. And the Chinese government did the right thing in supporting vocational education because China, more than ever, needs workers with skills to compete with the rest of the world.

CHAPTER TWELVE

I met another young man who came crying one day to see me. "What is this all about? Why are you crying?"

He told me a typical story of a bonsai kid. "My mother didn't think I should go to study in Australia. 'With that amount of money we will spend for you in Australia, we could buy you an apartment for your future,' they said."

"I see. What did your father have to say about it?"

"My father encourages me to follow my heart."

"I want you to go home this weekend and the three of you to sit down and discuss this," I suggested to him.

"Steve, we do not do that in China."

Bonsai kids are not allowed to have a mind of their own. I understood that. Parents' wish or desire is like a mandate from the heavens. And their task is to do what they are raised to do.

"You do that this weekend. That is why you are in college. You should learn to *negotiate* with your parents, OK?"

I assumed this was his first exposure to the word *negotiate* because the China I came to know does not encourage or use negotiation with their offspring. That is why I call or label them "bonsai kids" because they are grown, raised, pruned, and designed by their parents like a gardener toward his bonsai tree. They are not allowed to think independently. They are to do what they are raised to do—to follow the wishes of the person who has raised them up like a bonsai tree.

"Go home and negotiate with your parents," I insisted. "Why are you in college if you are not able to negotiate with your professors, boyfriends, girlfriends, government officials, traffic police, hawkers, and your own parents?"

So I told him what to say, especially to his mother. The bonsai kids in China are not trained or encouraged to speak to their parents and elders. That was my sad conclusion after working with them for seven years in mainland China. They were not trained to speak to or negotiate with their parents or anyone in a position of authority. A nation of parasites?

"Mom and Dad, you have taken very good care of me all my life. You gave me everything to send me to the best schools from elementary to junior to high school. And now I am about to finish my college. I want to further my education in Australia because, with an advanced degree, I could work for a big international company or a multinational here in China and have a better future. If you allow me this opportunity to study in Australia, when I return, I will have a good-paying job. And I will have the money to buy you one apartment or two or three. But you must allow me to pursue my dream now."

I had no idea what he said to his parents. After graduation, he was on his way to Australia.

Bonsai kids must learn to love their parents and also to follow their every wish. As the only child, they are expected to love their fathers and mothers. All I want for them is to learn how to negotiate in life to achieve their goals and dreams.

CHAPTER THIRTEEN

Who are the bonsai kids? In my personal desire to learn more about this new breed of kids, I did have the opportunity to *meet* a young Chinese college student who happened to appear on an American TV show during my first year in China. He was picked to represent the modern youth of China for this particular documentary show about the modern youth around the world. And I did not ask him how he was the lucky one to be picked. There was nothing unusual about this young man to distinguish him from millions, and he did not come from one of the cosmopolitan cities in China. In fact, he was going to an unknown little university somewhere in northern China.

Many Americans were impressed with his story because he had said the first thing he would do after graduation from college was to make enough money to buy a new apartment for his parents. The parents were ordinary farmers. Americans thought that was something unusual and amazing because most young American people would not say that.

In China, young men are expected to take care of their parents, the essence of Chinese filial piety. *Filial piety* is absent in our American vocabulary. In one strange way, Chinese bonsai kids are envious of the American kids because of their freedom to care or not care for their parents, their freedom to move out of their birds' nests once they finish high school. Chinese parents, like the Italians, want their kids to live with them forever. I should know that because I have lived in America for over a few decades. And I am also Chinese.

I had the opportunity to know this young Chinese man after his appearance on an American TV show through email. One American businessman in particular wanted to do something for him, and so when he went to China to inspect a factory; he had invited this young man to be his translator. The young man majored in English. I would always remember what he shared with me about what happened in the city where the factory was.

"You know, Steve, I have heard many stories about factories and migrant workers in China. And here I am, helping this American businessman as a translator visiting this one factory. Of course, he has heard many stories, good and bad, about factory conditions in China, and he is here to find out the truth for himself. In fact, many American reporters had come and pretended to be potential buyers with hidden cameras and recorded the inside conditions of some factories for the world to see. The truth is this one particular factory is prepared for his visit. But still, the many things I see are not good at all."

He continued, "I thank God that my parents sent me to college. In fact, I was the only boy in the whole village who went to college. I thank my parents for giving me a college education. And I do not have to suffer the same fate as these many unskilled young migrant workers from different parts of rural China, many now working in these factories. You have to be here to see what I am seeing. Some rooms do not have ventilation at all. Lighting is very poor everywhere inside the factory. Imagine the young boys and girls, most are in their teens, having to breathe the fumes from toxic materials in the air the whole day. There are so many chemicals used in this factory, and workers are breathing fumes from chemicals in rooms with no proper ventilation. Ventilation is the biggest problem in this factory."

I could feel his deep concern and anxiety while listening to his story. He continued, "And then to meet certain production deadlines, the workers have little sleep. They do not even have time to sit down to have regular meals. They have no time to relax. They cannot afford to get sick. And sometimes they are not paid on time. Nobody cares about their complaints. 'You don't like the work? You can go. There are thousands waiting outside the gates to come in.' Yes, we managed to talk to some workers away from the factory boss and managers. I have no idea what the American businessman is going to decide about his relationship with this particular factory. It is bad, Steve. I feel sorry for all the young men and women working here. What else can they do? They are from the rural areas in China. They know nothing. They have no education. They have no technical skills. Factory work is the only thing they can do. They have no other place to go. They are the real migrant workers."

Before I came to teach in China in 2008, I too had seen documentaries on American television done by American reporters using hidden cameras about the terrible conditions inside some factories. And despite this exposure, many major American brands continue to do business with these factories. Why? Money. They can make more profits because of low labor cost.

In the twenty-first century, things are changing in China. We hear some factories are being closed down because of inflation and rising labor cost everywhere. One factor is that many migrant or rural workers are getting smart. They are not willing to work for you for a low pay. They did it once. And that was thirty, twenty, or ten years ago. You can say they were hungry for food and money and jobs. Not now, no more. They are getting smarter. Now they have more options available to them. And with their savings, many are opening up their own small businesses everywhere they live. Now factories are vying for the few workers out there. Rising labor costs are also driving some foreign companies to move to other countries with much cheaper labor costs than China.

And with major improvement in transportation, especially the major highways linking all the growing cities across China, it is predicted that less people will have to travel long distances to find a job, and that means there will be less migrant workers seeking work in faraway places, leaving their children in the care of their grandparents. Things are changing fast in mainland China.

CHAPTER FOURTEEN

One summer out of curiosity when I was home in America in Washington State, I went to one Walmart store to see for myself what products are still made in China. It is a known fact for most Americans, rich or superrich, that Walmart is the shopping mecca for millions, with relatively lower or cheaper prices than other traditional stores or business outlets across America. Most Walmart stores in America cover a few acres of land with a large area devoted to parking, whereas in mainland China spaces are limited, and instead of spreading out, most Walmart stores are going up like high risers because there is no room horizontally. I shopped at a few Walmart stores in China, and you went from floor to floor to get what you want. Some of these stores are sandwiched in between other businesses. Walmart stores in America have the luxury of plenty of land to spread out with huge parking lots in front of them. Not so in China.

For years, the majority of American shoppers go to Walmart stores, looking for cheap products made in China. In China, an American reporter from a major TV network talked to Chinese shoppers in a Walmart store and found that many shoppers would go there looking for products made in America. Most Chinese prefer foreign products because they believe they are well made and durable and can be trusted. This will account for the number of Chinese tourists going to Japan annually to visit and shop. Japan and China are neighbors geographically. To many of them, Japanese-made products are still superior than those made in China, especially in the area of electronics and many simple household products.

And when I visited the Walmart store in my neighborhood once, almost all the products came from mainland China. The picture is different now. Now I see products from India, Philippines, Vietnam, Laos, Cambodia, Korea, Japan, and some countries in South America. Not everything now is made in China. With the labor costs going up each year, more and more products are being made in countries with much more competitive labor costs than China. And shockingly, for example, America is trying to make some of the products themselves because of the rising cost in China and reopen some factories on American soil. Interestingly, some American factories are owned and run by Chinese from mainland China. Some American workers are complaining about the Chinese work ethic. Chinese workers work too many hours; American workers complain.

And President Xi Jinping is saying we should not depend too much on foreign trade now but rather focus on developing our own domestic market, which is the biggest one in the world. China's **GDP** remains steady. The double-digit growth of past decades seems to have temporarily vanished, and the International Monetary Fund (IMF), at one point, is predicting that India could possibly perform better than China. I doubt it will ever happen because China has better infrastructure than any country in the world, especially backward India. India just recently signed to build the Chinese (not British or Japanese) speed trains across India. It is a fact that India does not have an attractive, workable international airport, not to mention the old highways that were there since August 15, 1947, when India ceased to exist as a British colony.

Infrastructure is a critical, indispensable key to one country's economic growth and expansion. That is why China's Belt and Road Initiative is in many parts of the world now. With improved infrastructure, we can see more Chinese goods coming to your neighborhood sooner than later. Also, China will acquire more raw materials from the less developed countries. It is a win-win strategy for all involved in the Belt and Road Initiative.

As of this writing, the China-Laos Railway just opened for business, allowing mainland China to expand to Southeast Asia—Thailand, Vietnam, Cambodia, Malaysia, and Singapore.

CHAPTER FIFTEEN

In Peking University, only students who score the highest in Gaokao, China's national college entrance examination, are admitted to this prestigious institution of higher learning in mainland China. A member of the elite C9 League of Chinese universities, analogous to the Ivy League schools in America, it was established as the Imperial University of Peking in 1898 with a royal charter by the Guangxu emperor. With its core values of "freedom of thought, embrace of diversity," it has educated generations of famous scholars, politicians, entrepreneurs, and innovators who have profoundly shaped China's modernization and advancement of knowledge. And when it celebrated its 120th anniversary in 2018, the university launched its ambitious global excellence strategy (with focus on CLOUDS, an acronym for "creativity, leadership, openness, uniqueness, diversity, and shaping"), ushering in a new era of international development.

But there was trouble in paradise. The headlines in the newspapers in 2011 told a different story. The university was attempting to do something with some *troubled* bonsai kids who might need some assistance to better their chances of success as a student. If this were to happen in an Ivy League school in the United States or in any American institution of higher learning, I doubt anyone would be concerned to accuse the university of deceit and other ulterior motives other than to make available psychological services to any student who might need some counseling or other assistance when confronted with personal, social, or academic issues as students. But here in China, before the school could implement a "consultation" program to assist the students, two British newspapers started accusing Peking University of trying to take away the freedom of students to be themselves. Both newspapers were from the United Kingdom, trumpeting their concerns or suspicions. One was the *Guardian*, saying, "Chinese students screened for 'radical thoughts' and 'independent lifestyles,'" and the other was the *Telegraph*, stating, "Peking University to screen students for 'radical thoughts.'"

I must be very naive or what. Both newspapers jumped into conclusion before the university had fully implemented the consultation program despite what the university had said was their reasons for wanting to adopt and implement it. According to the information from Peking University, the consultation program was initiated for a targeted group of students in November 2010 at the Health Science Center (PUHSC) and Yuanpei College by the Office of Student Affairs, the Office of Educational Administration, and the PUHSC Office of Education. Peking University planned to roll out the program to the entire campus in 2011.

In response to a reporter's question—what's the original intention of the consultation program?—the deputy director of the Office of Student Affairs had this to say:

> It is the educators' obligation to care for every student and create an environment for their healthy growth. It's a pity that a few PKU students encounter such difficulties in their studies that they cannot complete their credits or even drop out. Long-accumulated, comprehensive, and complicated reasons result in poor academic performance which cannot be solved by students themselves. The university should extend a

helping hand and mobilize all possible resources to give those students concern and guidance and carry them through. This is the original intention of the program.

The consultation work means when students encounter difficulties hard to overcome by themselves and even teachers engaged in the students' work, the schools and departments should invite teachers from teaching and educational administration, counseling and logistic service or even specialists off campus, to make a comprehensive analysis and scientific assessment of their academic performance and prepare support programs with a clear target.

It should be pointed out that the consultation means neither control nor punishment on students. On the basis of the current working mechanism at PKU, the consultation aims to further integrate resources and increase spending to improve our service level for students and help them get through. The key is to combine educational management and care, addressing psychological and practical problems overcoming academic difficulties, and solving other problems to show our care and love for students. For the students to be consulted, it provides an important opportunity to communicate with their teachers and improve their own plan for studies.

We are aware that the original intention and key of the consultation program is for students. What kind of students will benefit from the program?

So who were the bonsai kids who might truly benefit from the program? The university listed ten specific groups of students that sparked and started the controversy. According to the deputy director of the Office of Student Affairs:

> The focus is mainly on students encountering difficulties in their studies, and also on all the students in need of care and help. Based on experiences, we classify these students into 10 categories: students with radical thoughts, psychological fragility, poverty, registration changes, eccentricity, interpersonal communication, internet addiction, job difficulties, serious illnesses, and discipline violations.
>
> We've noticed that some students have radical thoughts or bigoted character, encountering difficulties in interpersonal communication, social adaptiveness, and their studies. They cannot analyze and handle their problems in daily life in a rational and manifold way. For example, they cannot get on well with roommates, cannot handle love setback in a calm way, and cannot adapt to career life after graduation. Extreme events happening on campus like Ma Jiajue's case have taught us bitter lessons. All of the problems cannot be solved just by an instructor or a single unit. Instead, it needs multilateral consultations, the counselors of which could include parents and security departments on campus. Some extreme events may be avoided if we give the students psychological guidance and emotional care to solve practical problems as early as possible.

As a college professor myself, what happened to the students in Peking University was not exclusively Peking's problems. They happened everywhere in almost every university in America, in Japan, in China, and also in Singapore. Students are humans, no different from the migrant workers or people like you and me around the world.

And the reporter continued with this question: "We have heard that the trial program is near its ending. Judging from so far, what is the effect?"

The answer was, "Some students overcame difficulties and returned to the orbit of studying. We find it necessary to build the consultation program after a series of successful examples because it's satisfactory in efficiency and effectiveness in solving problems."

The deputy director then shared the success stories of a student addicted to the internet who asked for consultation. Another student had to quit school because of a psychological problem, having difficulties with his studies and failing in his exams. Both students were able to resume their studies after the consultation.

The interview ended with the school saying, "Therefore, next we'll listen to the opinion of teachers, students and the society in a more active way to do better for the students' growth and success." The university sought suggestions from anyone who had ideas for improvement by giving out their phone number.

A response by the deputy director of the 21st Century Education Research Institute in Beijing was totally uncalled for when he said, "College students are all young and energetic, it is normal for them to have differentiated, active thoughts. It is their right to be radical. If a university punishes this, this university is morally degenerating. The university is somewhere to cultivate people's independent personalities and thinking, so it's totally wrong for Peking University to intervene in students' freedom to express their different opinions."

Reading his remarks caused my blood to boil because it seemed to me this man knew nothing about the types or kinds of students we have in our campuses today. Students are no different from ordinary people in society. If you care to look, there are problems everywhere in our society today. And the university is doing the right thing by helping those who need assistance and counseling.

Also, we cannot be blind to the fact that there are a number of students who should not be in school but are there because their parents believed so and not in training or vocational schools, learning some useful skills. Not all students, to me, are meant to be college students, a fact that is denied by almost all Chinese parents. Not so in America or in Germany, where many young people attend vocation training schools, coming out with skills respected and admired by society.

I had a simple question for this man: would a prestigious university like Peking University do something to destroy, belittle, and tarnish its reputation by doing something so unprofessional, unethical, and naive? I doubt that. On the other hand, I also believe any major institution of higher education has the right to do what they think are best for the well-being—be it psychological, social, personal, economic, or academic—of their students. Who are we to question their integrity and mission or motives in what they do or plan to do for the good of the whole within their institution?

Having lived and worked in China, the biggest tragedy to me is that many students in my campus are going through many struggles and problems but have no one to turn to for guidance. That to me is more tragic than a famous school like Peking University trying to do something to help their students find solutions to their problems. Most bonsai kids in mainland China just learn to accept or tolerate problems in their lives, which is so different from America. American students are not afraid to talk about their problems or try to find help wherever they can, first within their campus and then outside. American students are more at ease with discussing personal problems with friends and their teachers. This is not true in China partly because most Chinese teachers I know prefer to keep a distance between them and the students. They feel and believe they are paid to teach, not to listen to their moans and groans. They have deliberately built a thick wall, making it difficult for students to come to them for any kind of help, personal or academic. Sadly, many students also do not trust their friends and roommates about their personal matters because they do not want to lose face in their eyes partly because many bonsai kids are taught to be self-reliant and not dependent on others for help of any kind. So here in the campus, they do just that: they do not seek help, just learn to tolerate their own problems.

In fact, I read something in the news in China at the beginning of a new school year about one university requiring or demanding all incoming freshmen to sign a document to the effect that should they try or want to commit suicide, for whatever reasons, the school is not responsible for their actions. Maybe that is what Peking University should do too, free themselves from any kind of blame or obligation to the students, allowing bonsai kids to do what they want as responsible young adults. Having an old retired professor living in the dormitories to help students with their studies and problems would be a great service to the university.

CHAPTER SIXTEEN

So who is this person by the name of Ma Jiajue that Peking University alluded to? I did some research on Ma Jiajue and came across this headline on March 17, 2004: STUDENT KILLER AN INTROVERT WHO FINALLY CRACKS. I eagerly read the report not once but several times, and I felt deep sadness in my heart. How could the world be so heartless and cruel to this boy, ignoring and neglecting him when he was desperately in need of someone who would listen to his woes and sorrows? He had difficulty connecting with other human beings in his daily life.

On the other hand, it did not surprise me because it is also happening on American soil. What happened to Ma Jiajue in China is also happening in my own backyard, so to speak. Americans are no different in the way they treat children with similar problems facing Ma Jiajue in mainland China.

According to the report, at age eighteen, he ran away from school because he feared he might not pass the Gaokao. At age twenty-three, on his final year as a biochemistry major at Yunnan University, he committed a heinous crime and confessed to the police that he had killed four fellow students, the bodies found in the dormitory closets. He told the police that the boys had accused him of being a cheat in a card game. In the words of the report, "A loner at home; an introvert at school; a bookworm with a complex about his poverty; a kung fu fan who loved violent movies; and a brilliant student whose performance would suddenly dip."

A complex portrait emerged based on conversations with his parents, teachers, and peers. Coming from an impoverished rural family in a remote village, his longtime depression and introverted character might have contributed to his murder of four students. He had no close ties with two sisters and an elder brother, growing up lonely because his parents were preoccupied with farming. Both he and his father were men of few words. They seldom communicated with each other.

In primary school, he had few friends to play with. In junior high school, he became a top student and won second prize in the national physics competition, winning the admiration of his classmates, but he had no friends. In high school, he stayed aloof from his classmates and became addicted to kung fu novels. An inferiority complex because of his family's poverty added to his loneliness, and his academic performance suffered.

Obsessed with the possibility of failing to enter college, he ran away but returned to the campus resolved to work harder and gained university admission. In his first year in college, he tried to be sociable but failed, always picking fault with others, quarrelling with classmates, becoming more testy. He avoided group activities for four years, and classmates distanced themselves from him.

A psychology counselor at Renmin University of China in Beijing (another elite school in China) believes that university teachers should look out for mental problems in students and encourage them to participate in more collective activities to help overcome social problems. Violence in movies and on the internet should partially be blamed for rising crimes among young people. Ma Jiajue loved action movies, like many other college students, and surfed the internet for information about murders and attacks against the police.

It is a known fact that college students suffer psychological problems in various degrees. In 2003, a report said that around 16.5 percent of five hundred thousand Beijing college students have a "tendency towards illness." The article on Ma Jiajue concluded by saying, "To address the serious problem as many as 70 percent of Beijing-based colleges and universities have established psychological consultation centers to provide students with access to professionals to discuss their conflicts and issues." This was in 2004, way before Peking University initiated the consultation program in 2011 for students who needed help.

When a crisis like Ma Jiajue happened, the community or the nation would suddenly become reflective and critical of themselves. How come nobody came to help the student? All is not well in paradise with the bonsai kids.

CHAPTER SEVENTEEN

Right before a major national holiday in China, I asked one of my favorite female students where she planned to spend the holiday. Her simple quick response caught me by surprise: "I will be spending the holiday with my grandparents."

While the rest of the students in the class didn't think it was anything out of the ordinary, I wasn't sure if I heard her correctly. "Would you care to repeat what you just told the class?"

"I will be spending the holiday with my grandparents."

"I see." I was speechless. *What about your own parents?* I was tempted to ask but refrained from it. The students were correct: *This is China.* If I had lived long enough in China, I would have fully understood what the student said. The students understood what she said and what she meant because many of them were raised by their grandparents while their parents were away as migrant workers in major cosmopolitan cities across China.

But I was new in China; it was my first year in the country, and therefore, I was a little surprised by the response of this female student. Of course, my inclination was to ask her to explain to me or to the class her decision to spend time with her grandparents. I did not want to do it to avoid embarrassing her in front of her classmates. Young American people would tell you everything about anything but not the young people in China. You could say the Chinese youth are shy or hesitant when talking about something personal, like stories about their upbringing, their parents, and their families.

After I wrote my first book about my coming of age, my sister in the UK was very upset with me. "Why on earth do you have to tell the whole bloody world about yourself and our family? It is none of anyone's business. You should not be telling the world about us!" She was being Chinese.

"I am a writer," I told my sister, trying to appease her genuine anger at me. But I am also Chinese from head to toe.

My college students in China told me, "You have become too Americanized. You are not a Chinese anymore."

CHAPTER EIGHTEEN

Asian kids are a different breed. American host families were told not to hug the young Japanese people coming to America to spend their holidays. One of my son's classmates in college was a Japanese student. At dinner one evening at my residence, we talked about many things. Of course, as a parent myself, I was interested to learn more about his relationship with his parents. I asked him about what he would do if he saw his mother at the airport in Japan. "You know, in America, you would run and hug your mother."

"No, no, no, we do not do that in Japan," he said emphatically.

Like the Chinese, the young Japanese people are a different breed. European exchange students complained about being made or forced to drink milk, not beer or wine, in American homes. Different cultures, different habits. But what the female student said in class wasn't anything new to other Chinese students. "I will be spending the holiday with my grandparents."

I once read an interesting article in a women's magazine in America about the role of grandparents in the USA. It is a good idea to live close to your grandparents. Why? When your children are not happy with you, your ideas, or the way you do things, they can go to their grandparents for some relief instead of going to their friends. What do young people know about conflicts with their parents? It is like the blind leading the blind. But if they have their grandparents not too far away from them, they could go there to get away temporarily from their parents. They could always seek advice from their grandparents because they have many experiences raising their children.

I was impressed with the article and thought it is a good idea to live close to your grandparents. That is true in the USA. In China, grandparents are there for a different reason.

In China, grandparents have the responsibility to raise their grandchildren because the adult parents, especially those from rural areas, are away working in a city far away from home. Many bonsai kids are raised by their grandparents, especially those who live in nonurban areas in mainland China. Actually, the black grandparents in the United States of America play an almost similar role. But here in America, some black grandparents have no choice but to raise their grandchildren because many fathers or mothers are dead or heavily involved in crimes and drugs or languishing in jails for different crimes. *This is America.*

Another male student told me he would spend the same holiday with his grandparents. But he was happy and anxious to share with me his life story. I had a chance to teach him how to play the piano in my private apartment. He painted an interesting picture of his life with his grandparents.

"I have very little contact with my parents. They are migrant workers, busy somewhere in a big city in China. I was raised by my grandparents. Every time I return home for the holidays, my grandparents will spend money to go to the local market and buy my favorite meat, pork and beef," he told me privately. His grandparents did not eat much meat by themselves, but they would cook meat when the grandson was home for the holidays. He was raised by them since he was a baby.

This was something very new to me, something I was hearing for the first time in my life. Many parents would leave their homes in many rural areas and worked as migrant workers in some of the biggest cities

in China. And in the days and months to come, I would learn that many
of these parents would leave their children behind in rural areas, to be
raised by their grandparents. They would return home maybe once
a year, especially during the spring festival (*Chunjie*, in China) if they
could afford it. Many of these left-behind children would be raised by
their grandparents. Many grandparents would have difficulty raising
them as the children grew older; many of them would quit schools, and
the grandparents were too old to control or discipline them.

"In China," according to my student, "many parents would like to
bring their young children with them to work in some big cities. They
go there to make money because there is no job in the remote areas
where they come from. One thing I want you to know is something
called *hukou*, household registration system in our country. Right now,
my parents could not take me with them to a big city because of this
hukou. If I live and stay with them, because my *hukou* is in the rural
area, I will not receive any benefits if I go to any big city in China.
For example, I would not be allowed to attend a regular school for
city children because I come from a rural area. It is so sad but true.
Even my parents are not entitled to certain health-care services
because they have nothing to do with the national government.
They are administered by the local government. And so if you do
not have the local *hukou*, you are not entitled to any of their services.
And that is one big reason why my parents have to leave me with my
grandparents. I love my grandparents very much. I grew up with
them since I was a baby, and now I am going to college."

Then he shared with me a video of the family dog. "The dog in the
video now has five puppies. They were born recently when I was here
in the campus."

"I assume your grandma would keep one puppy and give the rest
away to her friends or neighbors," I said.

"No, my grandma will keep all of them."

"It would cost too much to feed them," I continued.

"No, we keep them for food."

"What do you mean?" I asked.

"Grandma would slaughter them for their meat."

"I see. You mean you eat dogmeat?"

I grew up very poor myself in Malaya (now Malaysia). We grew our own vegetables behind our house and would buy some fish from the fishermen who lived in our community. We would buy some pork, especially during the Chinese New Year. We raised our own chickens, but we might slaughter one or two during the Chinese New Year. And our folks might send one of our chickens as a gift to someone celebrating an important event. Growing up poor in a poverty-stricken farming community, any kind of meat was a luxury we could not afford, when most of us eked out our living from the soil, with no regular income from any other source in the community.

I understood my student when he told me his grandma would slaughter a dog for meat. I would also learn later that, in Guangxi, the province where his grandparents lived, people would eat dogmeat to celebrate the arrival of summer. This has been a longtime tradition and practice in this province in southern China, the home of my student and his grandparents.

Eating dogmeat, many believe, is good for your health. This tradition was started in the 1990s and now evolved into an annual dogmeat festival in Yulin, a city in this province, becoming one of the largest festivals in modern China. As a Chinese myself, I had no problem understanding the practice of eating dogmeat. But all is not well in Yulin as of this writing because many dog or animal lovers, growing in numbers in modern China because of their increased wealth, are staging some protests here and there, especially during the annual dogmeat festival in Guangxi Province. Traditions do not simply disappear because of protests by animal lovers.

I hear this joke often in China: many Chinese, especially those acquainted with drought, famine, and poverty, will eat anything that moves, including some of the four-legged animals. As a Chinese myself, nothing surprises me anymore. We will eat anything to survive, and throughout the long Chinese history, many of our ancestors suffered and starved because of drought and famine and constant fighting among local and regional warlords. Things changed, and life changed for the better after Chairman Mao Zedong founded the new communist China in 1949, marking the end of the dynastic rule and the short-lived republican rule. The China that most of us know today started in 1949.

And starting in early 1980s, with new economic reforms and the opening up of China to the West, many people found new opportunities to make a living by going to the big coastal cities in China, leaving many of their children in backward rural areas to their grandparents to raise them. So it did not surprise me that many of my students would talk often about their lives with their grandparents and not a word about their parents. I would say that most rural children are raised by their grandparents because, ever since the radical economic reforms and opening up of China to the world, many rural parents were able to find jobs in major cities along the coast. As they worked as migrant workers, many of them would return home once or twice a year, and many would build their two- or third-story houses in the countryside. Urban folks are not allowed to build their own houses, and thus, most of them now live in apartments in all the major cities in mainland China.

What an irony because only rural families are allowed to own land for cultivation and survival and also have the privilege to build their own houses. According to urban *hukou*, city dwellers are not allowed to own or cultivate any land. That privilege belongs only to rural folks across China.

CHAPTER NINETEEN

One day I was watching the news in China. It made me very sad. It was about a father and a mother who had decided to visit their son in some kind of camp for children addicted to computer games. Computer game addiction was a serious national disaster, a social problem that caught the attention of the central government in Beijing. Some bonsai kids are in trouble—now.

One of the first things that surprised me about China was how early many Chinese parents, anxious about the future of their only child, would expose their children to the use of computer. Many parents would spend enormous amount of money for their children to take classes in everything from A to Z, and learning the computer was one of such early endeavors. I saw young children exposed to different professions in China at an early age, like dressing up like a pilot and attending a class on what it means to be a pilot in modern China.

In America, where I live, students in high schools are now exposed to career paths with the assumption, I assume, that many would not go beyond high school. So they are preparing many high school students to the job opportunities after high school, instead of entering college life.

Little did some of the Chinese parents know that their sons, especially, would become addicted to playing computer games at an early age. Why did this happen? For this, you need to understand the educational system in mainland China. As early as primary school now, many children do not live at home with their parents. Almost all students live in dormitories across China. One reason is that most schools are in urban areas. Many parents are not aware that their sons, especially, would be playing computers, prohibited in their living quarters or dormitories, but they have the money to visit the nearest computer bars or cafés in many parts of China on weekends. That would account for many students becoming addicted to computers or computer games from a very young age.

I saw this TV report about a father and a mother now desperate to find a cure for their only son's addiction to computer. The parents finally took time off from their work as migrant workers somewhere in China, and they had decided to visit their son at this camp to see how well he was doing or progressing. Deaths were reported in this camp because of unscientific ways or methods of dealing with addiction. Harsh treatment was the main cause of death for some young people. Many parents were rightly worried because of reports of addiction in the news across China. At least they tried to send them to a camp for some kind of treatment.

Instead of talking to each other face-to-face, they sat side by side. The son was so angry at his parents that he refused to communicate orally with them. Instead, they were writing short notes to each other during the TV interview.

I will remember one thing the boy said to his parents: "Why are you interested in knowing how I am doing? Why bother to come and visit me here at the camp for those of us now addicted to computer games? You have been so busy all these years, and you did not have time to see me or talk to me, and now you want to see me. I am very angry at both of you. I do not want to talk to you."

It moved me to tears how angry he was at his parents. I totally understood his state of mind and the way he accused his parents of neglect. He felt they had abandoned him for years, working somewhere in a big city to make money so he could go to school. Now it appeared he was so angry that he refused to talk to his parents. I watched the bewildered parents sitting there, not knowing what to talk about or how to talk to their only son, who was now spending time in a camp for addicted children.

Would the boy ever understand why his parents had to leave him with his grandparents? Why they were busy making money so he could go to school and have a computer? Would the boy forgive them for abandoning him with his grandparents? It wasn't an easy decision for any rural parent at the time.

Back in my campus, they kept it a secret that one of our students had died after days and weeks of not eating but playing computer games. Most of us who live outside China are not aware of the fact that many junior and high school students do not live with their parents. They are starting with the elementary students in some places. Remember, about 50 percent of the people in China live in nonurban areas. There are no schools where they live, and they have to send their sons and daughters far away to attend schools in urban areas. And so their children will often live in dormitories in schools across mainland China. Those children with money might travel home on some weekends to see their parents, assuming they live not too far away from the schools. Most students will only see their parents during major national holidays when the schools are closed.

Though many or most high schools do not allow students to own or operate a computer in their dormitories, many of these students will spend their weekends at a computer bar or café near their campus, where they will spend their pocket money playing computer games and, in some cases, watch Japanese porn movies, though prohibited by law. And that is how many of these students, unbeknownst to their parents living far away from the campus, become addicted to computer games. Sad but true.

In China, most students are expected to spend hours daily doing their homework and always preparing for some kind of examination as long as they are students. While it is true there is time for everything, most students are expected to be with their books during most hours of the day, especially those living in the dormitories. All their after-school activities are strictly supervised by an adult, especially during study hours. There is very little time for recreation or any other personal leisure pursuits. So on weekends, they might escape to a local computer café or bar to play some computer games or to watch a Japanese porn movie. Remember, computers are not allowed in their high school dormitories, period.

Once, a college student shared with me what happened to his computer when he was home during one vacation from college. He was in a hurry to see a friend and left his computer on while he was gone. By chance, his mother saw the computer still running and found some Japanese porn movies in his computer. He got an urgent phone call from his mother to return home immediately.

"Is this how you spend your time in college? Watching dirty Japanese sex movies? Your father and I work hard to send you to college, and this is what you are doing?" His mother was very upset that he had Japanese porn movies in his computer.

"Ever since then, I had deleted all my Japanese sex movies from my computer. I do not want another lecture from my mother. She is my mom, and I want her to be happy with me and trust me when I am in college." He told me of this incident when he was home during a school break. This is the voice of a bonsai kid.

What is the truth? Do all Chinese students watch Japanese porn movies? Yes and no. Is the computer just for studies or games or Japanese sex movies? Or is the computer for all of the above for many male students in contemporary China?

After parents introduce the computer to their sons or daughters, they do not have the supervision or control of how their children will use it because most of them live in dormitories far away from home. And there are computer cafés and bars outside many of these dormitories across China. Most high schools do not allow students to bring computers to school dormitories for personal use. But computer bars or cafés are just outside the gates of these schools and dormitories. This is China.

CHAPTER TWENTY

I could only share what happened in my own apartment in China. A student spent an evening with me and saw a *Penthouse* magazine in my bedroom. It is a men's magazine that combines urban lifestyle articles and softcore pornographic pictorials that evolved into hard core. Founded in 1965 in the United Kingdom, it was sold in the United States starting in 1969.

One summer home in the USA, I made the decision to bring a few of the so-called men's magazines to China for a reason. A survey of more than ten thousand twenty-five- to thirty-four-year-olds in China, according to statistics from Durex Global Surveys by Durex.com, suggests that Chinese adults' first sexual experience has fallen from twenty-two in 2001 to eighteen in 2005. One of my students had introduced me to the Chinese Sex Culture Festival in the internet with the theme "healthy and harmonious sex" in Guangzhou, Guangdong Province, every year since 2003. I did not realize the communists are that liberal about sex or sexual practices in communist China. That was a surprise to me. Two eye-catching parts of the festival involved a lingerie fashion show and sex toy exhibition, which drew thousands of visitors, both young and old.

In the entry to the exhibition hall, there was a huge well-carved wooden phallus on display. There was also a bigger-than-life-size sex doll to attract visitors to the festival. It was so popular that organizers planned to hold similar festival in other parts of China. But this festival introduced many products including life-size sex dolls to the public but no sex magazines or sex movies for curious visitors. That was the reason why I decided to expose my male students to the men's magazine from America.

In fact, I told an American friend that "if a Chinese custom officer at the international airport in China finds the men's magazine [illegal in China] in my luggage, I would tell them I am using it to teach American culture to my students. And if they are not convinced of my bullshit, I would be happy to give it to them for personal pleasure." Chinese custom officers usually never bothered to check my luggage during my seven years in and out of mainland China because I looked like a college professor to them or someone who looked honest and like a gentleman. I could have carried an explosive, and they wouldn't know because they somehow trusted me.

The student, after studying the pictorials in *Penthouse* magazine, announced to me, "Steve, these girls are too fat and ugly to me."

"Oh, I am sorry," I said rather amusingly.

"I can show better-looking Japanese girls."

"Really?"

"Do you want to see them?"

"Why not?"

Poor, innocent me, I did not realize this student carried a few Japanese porn movies in his mobile phone, something shockingly new to me. I was naive or ignorant, a bookworm, not a sex maniac, all my life.

He said eagerly, "We could watch it together using your laptop."

Why not? I am not a fastidious kind of person but easy to please. And here is my sincere confession: for the first time in my life as an adult American, my Chinese student wanted me to see better-looking girls, those sexy Japanese girls in a Japanese porn movie. He did not like the females in my men's magazine. Maybe he was not used to seeing naked American or European women. He judged the *Penthouse* pictorials of females to be too ugly or fat or unattractive to him. Anyway, I was grateful for the opportunity to view a sex movie in the privacy of my own apartment. Why not? Seize every opportunity to learn from others, especially if I wanted to be a writer. I did pursue studies in journalism in college.

Another student told me, "When I was a little kid, my parents went to work one day, and I found a sex DVD in the house. And I watched a Japanese sex movie when I was a little boy." Are you kidding me? What? I could not believe my ears.

Ever since, I realized sex or sexual awareness is everywhere in China because any kid could download a Japanese sex movie if you could read and understand Chinese. They must have felt sorry for me because I did not know any Chinese, and I was not in the habit of downloading anything using my computer. After all, in my country of America, I could buy, as an adult, anything related to sex in a sex store. I never saw the need to download anything, and my preoccupation was education and knowledge, not sex.

My sad conclusion is that many of my Chinese students, both boys and girls, know more about sex than poor innocent me from America visually and vicariously, though there is very little sex education in Chinese schools from elementary all the way to college; thus, many suffer from sexual diseases and unwanted pregnancies across China. Commercial notices about abortion (killing a baby) are everywhere in major cities in mainland China. I wasn't aware of these notices because they were written in Chinese. But my students told me they are everywhere in the cities across China. Abortion in China is everywhere like ice cream is in the USA. I would soon learn "killing a baby" is pretty common in China.

Chapter Twenty-One

One day in the campus, a student came sobbing to me. "What is the problem?" I asked innocently.

"My girlfriend is pregnant," he said calmly.

"Pregnant?"

"We have decided to kill the baby," he said calmly.

"You mean abortion?" I said, trying to be calm like a tired cat.

I would soon learn that most people do not use the word *abortion*, but they would say "kill the baby" to me.

"I am sorry. I made a mistake," he continued calmly.

"No, it is not a mistake. It is called s-t-u-p-i-d-i-t-y," I said calmly, and I spelled out the word slowly for him, making sure he understood what I was trying to say to him. "So what can I do for you?"

"My girlfriend and I have decided to kill the baby. Could I borrow some money from you? At the beginning of next month, I will pay back the loan. Is that OK with you?" He said it calmly.

This would not be the first time a student or a working young adult would tell me they had to kill a baby because they did not like the feeling of using a condom. Not one but quite a few of them had shared this with me in private. And they said it calmly.

Most students could trust me with their personal secrets. To them, I am an American, not a Chinese. They will not share any personal secrets with their best friends or roommates. I find that to be a little baffling. What is more incredible is a student might say something like this to me when they visited me: "If you like, we can watch a movie together." Usually, it is a Japanese sex movie. They knew I do not read Chinese, and that prevented me from downloading any movie in China.

And that is why there are many places or rooms a student could use for one hour or two or three. I have never seen that in America all my life. Even some major big hotels advertise for a one-hour or two-hour service. That means sex is everywhere in China if you understand their culture and lifestyle. That is why some of my students feel at ease talking about Japanese sex movies with me. Now you know.

CHAPTER TWENTY-TWO

I was on my bicycle one day when I saw John right behind me. It was time for lunch, and we were going in the same direction, to the canteen in the campus. "What is up, John?"

"Don't call me John anymore," he replied angrily, like someone had punched him on his face.

"Oh dear, what is happening to you? Can we stop and talk for a minute?"

We found a place to sit, and I decided to find out what was going on with him that he did not want me to call him John anymore. "What happened to you? Why are you so angry at the moment?" I asked.

"She is not answering my phone calls. She does not love me anymore."

"Care to explain what is this all about? So your girlfriend is not answering your phone calls. Maybe she is busy with something. This is the beginning of a new school year. Maybe she is busy with some homework. Is that possible? John?"

"I know this is the beginning of our college life. And this is our first semester at the campus. When we were in high school, she and I would work together on her math because I was really good in math.

And she would cook something special for me to eat. She would even bake a cake for me."

"John, people do that all the time—I mean, cooking or baking something special for you to express their appreciation of what you did for them."

"Now I called her, and she did not answer my phone. She does not love me anymore."

Something came to me, and I asked John the most important question. I said, "When did she say 'I love you' to you?"

He was quiet for a minute, and he did not say anything to me.

"When did she say 'I love you' to you?" I repeated.

He was shaking his head.

"So she never did say it to you. She never did, but you assumed she did. You know, John, I am older than you, and I have learned something about life. Many times, we humans create problems for ourselves. Agree?"

He was quiet because he was thinking about what I had just said to him. We went to lunch together. He was his normal self the next time I saw him in the campus.

Many bonsai kids simply do not use their brains. If only they will learn to think. The Chinese school system does not teach creative thinking in their school curriculum. Blame the system. Most thinking are done by their parents, the creator of the bonsai kids.

CHAPTER TWENTY-THREE

I was in a computer classroom one day when a student came in to ask me if he could use a computer. "My parents are not sure if I need a laptop at the moment. So I do not own a computer. Is it okay if I use one to write something for my professor?"

"Of course. Our computers are for all students to use in the campus."

Something about the Chinese campus that the world could learn is that, once in a while I would meet a student who told me he was not a regular student in my class but who had the permission to *audit* the class, *panting* in Chinese. I thought it was a great idea. Not so in America when I was an international scholarship student. Maybe that experience might lead him to enroll in the class one day. Or someone was simply inquisitive and adventurous and eager to learn something new. But students did come to audit in my classes.

The young man who wanted to use a computer was not my student because he was pursuing a degree in political science. He was an ambitious young man and would like, one day, to work in a foreign embassy for the Chinese government. He loved to travel, he told me. And his English was fluent, though he was not an English major. That was very unusual to me. The irony was that some English major students, my students, were not articulate or fluent in their spoken English. Most students could write well but were unable to speak English fluently.

I would soon discover that some students felt uncomfortable speaking English to their fellow Chinese students. "We are Chinese, and it does not make sense for us to be speaking English." I agreed and also disagreed with this kind of thinking. Why bother to major in or study English if one has no desire to speak English as one way of communicating?

In fact, I learned during my first months in the campus which students could speak and write fluent English. It's not what you think. They were not English major students. I would soon discover that students who major in science and technology are the ones who are fluent in English. Why? Because these are the students who are aspiring to pursue higher and advanced education abroad. And they are smart enough to prepare themselves, mastering the English language while in high school and now in the university.

Also, they are students who want to work for big international companies or multinationals in China or in the diplomatic services for the Chinese government. And they are those who told me, "One day I want to travel around the world to experience different cultures myself." The student who came to the computer room was one such student. He wanted to join the foreign service for the Chinese government.

We became friends very quickly because of his ability to speak English with me. During my years in China, he would talk to me about some very personal problems with friendship, especially with those of the opposite sex. One of his first girlfriends was rejected by his mother. "My mother said her mouth is too big." It seemed funny at the time.

He became very serious with another female student. She was a student in business and economics and aspired to be a college professor. You would think this would please his mother. His mother told him in no uncertain terms that he must also drop her for a very strange reason as I would soon discover.

You have to live in China to understand this: most middle-class parents, especially those who have a steady regular income, would save and save for their only sons or daughters. So he told me his parents had planned to buy him an apartment. In China today, a girl might be interested to marry you if you own an apartment. Or the girl's parents might not be interested to talk to you if you do not own an apartment in China. This is an indisputable fact of life in modern China. No apartment, no marriage—plain and simple.

So what was the problem with this ambitious new female friend? She made the mistake of asking and insisting that her name be on the deed of the new apartment. That is an absolute no in China because the boy's parents do not trust you enough to believe you will marry her son for love, not for his apartment. A new law in China also makes it clear that if the apartment belongs to a man or woman before the marriage, it will not be part of the divorce settlement. But the mother of my student did not want to gamble with the new law; she simply told her son to drop her. The mother was not willing to negotiate with the son's new girlfriend.

One Friday night, he came to visit me. And I asked him where his girlfriend was. By then, he had a different girlfriend.

"Steve, I do not know what to do anymore. I do not want to spend any time with my girlfriend. She asks me to jump, I jump. She asks me to eat, I eat. But now she does not want me to talk to any girls in my class. It is so ridiculous. I was out jogging the other night with a few of my classmates including a few females. She hung up on me and told me to stop jogging with them. She is so impossible. I do not know what to do with her."

To me, it was a simple problem requiring a simple solution, not an easy one for just anyone. So I tried. "Tell me, are you married to her? Yes or no."

"No," the student said.

"She is not married to you, and you are not married to her. You are free to do what you want. Agree?" It is very simple logic to me. But human relationships do not adhere to any kind of logic most times.

Then I said the most ridiculous thing to him. "Why are you letting this girl control you? Why? You are upset because you let her control you. Does that make any sense to you?"

"What do you want me to do?"

"You can stop it right now. You are not married to her, and you are not obligated to her. You are a free man. Does that make any sense to you?"

Soon their relationship was over. Good for him.

But his mother continued to tell him what to do when it came to choosing a girlfriend or a future wife. The last girl he tried to introduce to his mother did not get her approval. "She is too ugly for you."

Finally, he and I sat down for a long talk. And I remember every word I taught him to say to his mother. She had some personal problems and left teaching before retirement age. Because he was not far away in school, he would return home on some weekends to be with his mother. He loved his mother, an obedient son.

I said to him, "Go home and sit down quietly over a cup of Chinese tea with your mother. And I am going to tell you what to say to your mother, OK? It goes something like this. 'Mom, all these years, you took care of me and gave me everything I would ever ask for. You want always the best for me. You sent me to the best schools. You supported everything I did in my life. I would soon graduate and work for the government if I pass the civil service exam. I know I would do well because I am one of the best students in the university. I am here to talk to you about something that is very important to me. I have to choose a wife, someone I would have to live with twenty-four hours a day. I believe you should allow me to make this decision because I am old enough to know what is best for my life and my future. It is time that I must make the decision to choose the girl I want to marry. I hope you will try to understand me. You must allow me to make this important decision for myself and my life. I know you will always be there for me.'"

I tried very hard to avoid saying this to the mother: "You will not be able to take care of me forever, and so I must make some critical decisions by myself and for myself." As a Chinese myself, this is not easy to tell my father or mother. The fact is they will not be able to take care of me forever.

Bonsai kids in China are not encouraged or allowed to discuss any matter with their parents. Children listen and obey their parents. Filial piety for your parents does not allow you to question your parents' decision concerning your life, career, or future wife. You do what you are told to do. It's that simple. I should know because I am Chinese myself.

Whether my student told his mother what I told him to say, I would never know. I did know one thing: he married the so-called ugly girl that his mother had rejected. During the few times I returned to China, this student would pick me up at the airport in his big SUV and took me out to eat in the best restaurants in town. He would entertain me and invited me to stay in his palatial apartment. I was happy for him. Was he making all the money working for the central government? I was curious, but I did not ask until something happened one day.

During one of my visits with him, he said to me out of the blue, "Steve, I do not have the time to see you this weekend because I have to go and visit my apartment."

My apartment? What apartment? Which apartment? I had stayed with him and his wife at the apartment.

"Oh, not that apartment. That was a gift from my wife's parents. Also, the big white SUV I was driving? That was a gift from my wife. Hm! I am trying to finish decorating my apartment my parents bought for me before I was married so we could rent it out."

"I see."

Whatever happened to his mother's objection to his ugly girlfriend, now his wife? I am curious.

CHAPTER TWENTY-FOUR

On December 7, 2017, I was home in America (I had returned home in 2015 after seven years as a visiting professor in China) when I saw the headlines: MEET US ON THE BROKEN BRIDGE IN 20 YEARS: CHINESE GIRL ADOPTED BY AMERICANS REUNITES WITH BIRTH PARENTS and MEET ME ON THE BRIDGE: DISCOVERING THE TRUTH ABOUT MY PARENTS AFTER 20 YEARS. It was a film by *BBC Stories*, filmed and directed by Changfu Chang.

It was a simple story about a little girl of about three days old when her parents, because of the one-child policy, was left in a market somewhere in China. Obviously, her birth as the second child would be considered illegal at the time in mainland China. The film focused on the girl, now twenty, by the name of Kati Pohler and how she discovered that her birth parents had left her a note that every year on the same day, they would wait for her on the famous Broken Bridge in Hangzhou.

I myself had the privilege to visit the famous West Lake and the Broken Bridge, a major tourist attraction in Hangzhou. So since 2004, Katie's father, Xu Lida, would return to the bridge on the same day as he had written on that special note left with the baby girl. He would scan the faces in the crowd, looking for the daughter he had given up long ago.

According to BBC, after marrying in 1992, Lida and his wife welcomed their first daughter and decided to have another child so the first one would not be lonely. (Many of my students told me they were lonely growing up without a little brother or sister.) That would violate the one-child policy and would result in harsh punishment like forced abortion, sterilization, loss of property, and steep fines, which the young couple could ill afford. The family planning officials demanded an abortion and threatened to destroy their home. But the young couple was determined to start a new life on the run to save the baby, even if it meant giving the child away. They hid on a boat, and a little girl was born. Three days later, they took their baby to a market and left her there with a kiss and a special note attached to her.

China began international adoptions in the early 1990s. A year after the young couple left the baby girl in a vegetable market, an American couple from Michigan, Ruth and Ken Pohler, adopted their daughter Kati from the Suzhou Social Welfare Institute. They found something a little unusual, a note attached to the baby written by Kati's birth parents, which ended with a passionate plea: "If God has sympathy for us and you care about us, let's meet on the Broken Bridge on the West Lake in Hangzhou on the morning of Chinese lunar date July 7th in 10 or 20 years."

The date is important because it is almost similar to Valentine's Day in China, July 7, a time for loved ones to meet and reunite. So when Katie turned ten years old in 2005, the Pohlers found a messenger through a friend and sent her to the Broken Bridge in Hangzhou on the appointed day as requested in the note. Kati's birth father was there, and by chance, a Chinese TV crew captured him on tape.

"Holding a sign. The name on the sign was the name in the note," said Changfu Chang, the filmmaker.

The messenger was able to find the birth parents because the story captivated a national audience. It was big news in China. But soon the messenger disappeared.

The Chinese parents were planning for a reunion. The Pohlers did let the birth parents know that Kati was well cared for in America. The birth parents continued their annual trip to the Broken Bridge on July 7 and feared their daughter might not want to see them or that they were being punished by God. The Pohlers kept the secret until Kati was twenty years old. Kati made the decision to go to the Broken Bridge in Hangzhou, China, to meet her birth parents on the appointed day, July 7. She did. Was she happy to finally meet her biological parents? We will never know.

My instinctive reaction to the BBC film was predictable. It should be more than a film about the little girl and her discovery of her biological parents twenty years after her birth and why the young Chinese couple gave her away with a kiss and a note attached. To me, the focus of the film should be about why China was forced into adopting the one-child policy and its consequence of forcing many Chinese parents to decide their preference for males because of a strong Chinese tradition that the boys will carry on the family name and will take of their parents when they grow old. It was against the law in China to have a second child.

If I was the filmmaker, that was what I would have done, focusing on Kati and her biological Chinese parents in mainland China. If she had been told the truth about this reunion, Katie could have studied more Chinese to prepare her to meet her biological parents. Watching the film, it was obvious to anyone that Kati was very uncomfortable because she was not fluent in Chinese and was unable to communicate with her little sister and her biological parents. I believe the outcome would have been very different if she had mastered the Chinese language during that ten-year waiting period before being told the truth about her biological parents and their sincere desire to meet their daughter at the Broken Bridge in Hangzhou, China.

CHAPTER TWENTY-FIVE

Once back on American soil after seven years in China, I made the quick but critical decision to talk to Americans, especially whites, about my front-row, firsthand experiences living and working in China. Why? Because once I had the privilege of living and working in China and having many rare opportunities to spend time with the parents of my college students and those outside the campus, I began to see and understand China very differently, more objectively if that was possible.

Most tourists do not have that privilege of knowing China as intimately as I did. Having lived in the United States of America first as an international scholarship student and later as a citizen, most Americans—young and old, educated and uneducated, rural and urban—are simply disinterested in what is happening within mainland China, roughly the same size as the country of the USA. One could easily blame China for not doing enough to *sell* mainland China and its rich culture, traditions, and practices to the world, like the Japanese are doing through many of their NHK TV programs. Japan is mighty proud of its beliefs, practices, traditions, and culture. Why is modern China not doing it using the mass media around the world? I believe China could and should do more via their CGTN TV network like what the Japanese are doing now.

Nevertheless, much have been written about the old and new China by many outsiders, China watchers and scholars. Anyone interested can always obtain a copy of a book about China. *This Is China* is my first 527-page book about my experiences living and working in mainland China, and I am using it to share my rich experiences with Rotary International club members in Washington State, where I now reside.

Why the Rotary International clubs? When I was an international scholarship student in America, I was invited to talk about Southeast Asia and the unpopular Vietnam War then because I came from Singapore, which is not too far from the country of Vietnam. I had spoken to quite a few Rotary International clubs since I came to the USA. That is the reason why I made the decision now to return to the Rotary International clubs and share my seven-year experiences living and working in mainland China.

Prodigal Son is my first fiction about a wealthy but immoral college student in mainland China, which is based on many private and personal stories my students had unabashedly shared with me at the dinner table of my apartment near the campus in China. In fact, one day while I was waiting for my annual car checkup at a car dealer here in my hometown of Puyallup, Washington State, I saw a white gentleman also waiting for his car, and he was reading a thick, fat book, a science fiction by a Chinese writer in mainland China. As a writer, I had to ask him about his interest. He was happy to show me the cover of the book but did not want to go any further with our casual conversation. I did manage to give him my business card with a list of the eight books that I had authored thus far. When I tried to talk to him about modern China, he told me he preferred to read his book and abruptly returned to reading.

You could say that is what many Americans will do; they are not interested in hearing more about China from me, someone who had the privilege of spending seven years as a visiting professor in China. In my public speech to Rotary International clubs, I tried not to say too much about China without being accused of being pro-China.

"What I am sharing with you today is based on my experiences living and working in mainland China." It is none of my business to tell my suspicious audience that China will take over the world sooner than later. History is our witness to this momentous event.

You might just be surprised how I continue to get myself invited by Rotary International clubs, say, within a radius of two hundred miles from my residence in Washington State. First, I went to the internet and tried to send an email to someone within the club who might be responsible for the club's activities. And the email would include this brief introduction:

> **Title of the talk**: One American's Perspective of Modern China
>
> **Name of speaker:** Stephen Ling
>
> **Email:** stephenehling@hotmail.com
>
> **Facebook:** www:facebook.com/stephenehling
>
> **WeChat ID:** 1962816801
>
> **Brief description of the talk:** It is imperative for the world to understand and appreciate what is happening inside mainland China today because China is on the rise, especially economically. My sixth book, *This Is China*, is my endeavor to share my seven-year stint in China as a visiting professor (2008–2014); my firsthand, front-row experiences of what life is like inside China. I wrote *Speaking English*, two textbooks for use by university English major students in mainland China. *Prodigal Son* is my first novel about modern China.

Bio: I grew up in Malaysia in a poor farming family. My grandparents hailed from Fujian Province, China. From an early age, I knew education is my key to salvation and out of poverty. Eventually, I got scholarships to study in the USA. I had three dreams and achieved them all: be an author, be a college professor, be a talk show host in China.

About my books:

This Is China: "A colorful, bicultural journey" (*Kirkus Reviews*).

"Stephen is passionate, open and articulate" (Prof. Zhuang Hongming, chairman, School of Journalism, Xiamen University, China).

Growing up Chinese: "Overall, this memoir is action-packed and often engaging" (*Kirkus Reviews*).

"The book's pace is quick and smooth. Ling's tone is open and inviting, even as it carries the tension, agitation, and energy of his youth" (Clarion Reviews)

Crazy Americans: "Stephen writes with passion and flair" (Dr. Junid Saham, director, Areca Capital, Malaysia).

Prodigal Son: "An exciting first novel about a rich but decadent youth in modern China" (Dr. Alex Qi Song, Harvard University).

Letter to Fellow Immigrants: A Memoir: "A fascinating read for those who believe or doubt the American dream" (Assunta Ng, publisher of *Northwest Asian Weekly*).

Bonsai Kids: Work in progress about how Chinese parents raised their children of the one-child policy (1980–2015) like a gardener would his precious bonsai tree.

My early attempts to introduce myself to the Rotary clubs via email did not work, much to my surprise. I waited for weeks, and there was no response. And so I came up with a simple idea: invite myself to their luncheon meetings, armed with a simple business card to introduce myself.

I must say it was a huge success judging from the responses of the club members to my presence. In some cases, they would not allow me to pay for my own lunch. In some cases, they would allow me to say a word or two on why I was there. I got the impression that one has to be invited by a member to attend a meeting.

And as I had planned and anticipated, over 80 percent of the clubs would invite me to share my American perspective of modern China. I was not there to sell any of my books, but autographed copies of *This Is China* are available if they so desired.

I continue to write three different columns in my Facebook account: one Chinese's perspective of the world, one Chinese's perspective of China, and one Chinese's perspective of America. Eventually, I hope to publish a book, essentially a compilation of what I have written and continue to write in my Facebook: one Chinese's perfective of America, China, and the world. Why not?

CHAPTER TWENTY-SIX

Like it or not, most Americans lack genuine interest in mainland China. During one summer break, I took a graduate student guest from mainland China to a local public school here in the USA; and to my profound embarrassment or dismay, the American students could not point out on a big world map the location of modern China. I do not expect the ordinary American citizen to know where China is on the world map either.

I took every opportunity to tell my American friends that the word *China* does not exist on the Pacific-centered map commonly displayed and used in the schools in today's China. We Americans are used to the Atlantic-centered map of the world (commonly called *Euro-centered map*), where we see the USA on the left, facing Europe on the right. In the Pacific-centered map, mainland China is in the center, facing the USA on the right. *Middle Kingdom* is the word for China on the Pacific-centered map. In ancient China, they built the famous Great Wall to keep out the outsiders, invaders, or barbarians, and the emperors demanded homage to his kingdom while sitting in the middle of his world, thus the name Middle Kingdom, located right in the middle of the then known world. You will not see the Atlantic-centered or Euro-centered map anywhere in mainland China today, maybe in the American Embassy or in some of the American businesses or agencies operating in China.

To understand China, you must first shift the way you see or perceive China or the Middle Kingdom in the center of the Pacific-centered map. In the old Euro-centered map, common everywhere in the USA, China exists in the Far East. It is still in many college textbooks. It is not in the center as in the Chinese map. The two maps tell a different story of the importance of the Middle Kingdom in the world in the past and in the future.

One common excuse for the ignorance or indifference about the existence of China is that America is the biggest and most important or admired country in the world. "Why should we be interested about China? We have everything here, and we do not need anything from China." That was what the emperors in mainland China once thought about the barbarians or outsiders trying to impress them with foreign gifts. China was way ahead than any civilization in the world then. Any wise students would know the list of inventions found in China. You could say the emperors were very arrogant then for many good reasons and did not welcome the bribes or gifts from foreign powers trying to break the ice or do business with them.

Foreign powers did to China what the early Americans did to the West Coast, pushing from the original thirteen colonies on the East Coast, fighting against or subjugating any powers or entities that stood in their way toward a manifest destiny to become the America of today. You wonder why modern China is so suspicious of Western powers today and chooses to mind their own business, hoping the rest of the world will also strictly adhere to its five principles of peaceful coexistence since 1954: "mutual respect for sovereignty and territorial integrity; mutual non-aggression; non-interference in each other's internal affairs; equality and mutual benefit; and, peaceful coexistence."

Why is the United States of America so obsessed with what China is doing for its country and trying to promote win-win economic panaceas and infrastructure improvements around the world, especially through President Xi's very successful, far-reaching Belt and Road Initiatives around the globe? We do not care about China because the USA has everything? True and not true. Summer is about over now in America, and many department stores are preparing for the coming fall. In fact, one could see all the new, bright, and colorful products on the floors and shelves mostly labeled Made in China. Yes, once it was Made in Japan; now it is Made in China. Former president Donald Trump failed to decouple the USA from China economically during his four-year failed experiment in the White House. Most Americans decided not to hire him again to run the country.

A smart person knows we live today in an interdependent world. An American friend in the state of Ohio recently emailed me to say he had no choice but to buy products made in China for his yard. "China offers me variety of products for my garden, and the prices are very reasonable compared to our American same products!" Amen. And that is the very reason why former president Bill Clinton worked hard to welcome mainland China into the WTO. In his mind, China's accession to the World Trade Organization or more trade with China would inevitably advance America's economic expansion and interests around the world. And China became a member of the World Trade Organization on December 11, 2001. Now products made in China are in every corner of the world.

But sadly and truthfully as of this writing, Americans are told and warned of the economic disaster awaiting all of us during the major holidays right around the corner because many container ships with goods from China and other parts of the world are not able to unload the products at the various ports. Americans must be prepared to pay higher prices for anything and everything related to our holidays. These ships are not able to "park" in New York or Los Angeles, and even if they could unload some of the containers, they could not find enough trucks and truck drivers to haul them to all the stores across the United States of America. We are in for trouble and should be prepared to pay for high and higher prices to get what we want for the holiday season. Because of the pandemic and the generous government stimulus checks and savings, more and more people here and around the world could not wait to spend their savings and money on things, things, things. And many of them are now sitting idly near the major ports of entry, both in the East and West Coasts of America.

CHAPTER TWENTY-SEVEN

Back home in America now, I have time to think about my seven years in mainland China, especially my time spent with the bonsai kids. When I was preparing to go to China as a visiting professor in 2008, the devastating massive Wenchuan earthquake took place in the mountainous central region of Sichuan Province on May 12, 2008. I immediately phoned my professor friend in Beijing, the capital of China, if he and his wife had said "I love you" to his son that morning before he left for school. He said, "We don't do that in China. My son knows that we love him."

Shortly after the earthquake, Reuters estimated that around nine thousand schoolchildren died, using numbers from reports by the state news agency and local media. Because of the one-child policy, many families lost their only child when schools in the region collapsed during the earthquake. Many schools in the earthquake zone crumbled, while buildings around them remained standing. Many young schoolchildren had died in schoolhouses called *tofu schools* because of the way they had crumbled under the tectonic onslaught.

According to some estimates, as many as seven thousand classrooms collapsed, and up to ten thousand students may have died. In all, nearly seventy thousand people died in the quake, and eighteen thousand were considered missing; officials now say those still missing are almost certainly dead.

Very few people knew that Shifang, the area near the epicenter of the Wenchuan earthquake, was a test case for the one-child policy. Population planners chose Shifang and used coercive methods to lower birth rates. They chose Shifang because it is the heartland of rural China and also home to a tenth of China's population. It is also the birthplace of Deng Xiaoping, successor to Chairman Mao. And by 1979 (the year before the launch of the one-child policy), Shifang's population had plunged drastically, and 95 percent of couples had pledged to have only one child. This gave the central government in Beijing a sense of tremendous possibility and a demographic miracle.

Tragically, when the Wenchuan earthquake struck in 2008, some eight thousand families—over two-thirds of which were single-child families— lost their only child. The earthquake had wiped out a generation in some villages. Families were pressured into signing documents pledging to keep quiet and not rock the boat, so to speak. It was the year of the Beijing Olympics. The central government forbade the media to write stories about the grieving parents and the shoddy school construction that had caused so many deaths of schoolchildren. Those who tried to ask questions or question the government were jailed.

Many Chinese still believe in omens and interpret a natural disaster, like the Wenchuan earthquake, as a sign of the withdrawal of the mandate from heaven from China's emperor or anyone in power. Could this earthquake be a judgment on the one-child policy? We will never know because we are mortal beings, not gods. Some suspected the construction of massive dams in highly seismic areas might have triggered the quake. It's pure speculation at the moment.

The Communist Party had worked long and hard to ensure the year 2008 would be associated with a glorious future for the nation, and not the deadly Wenchuan earthquake, in hosting the much-anticipated 2008 Beijing Olympics, the coming-out party of China to the world. All across China, clocks were set on a countdown to the day of the opening ceremony: 8:08 a.m., August 8, 2008.

CHAPTER TWENTY-EIGHT

After returning home to the USA in the summer of 2015, I have the time and luxury to focus on the young people in China, the bonsai kids, and continue to read and research on the contentious issue of the one-child policy, which the Chinese government was forced to adopt and implement in 1980. Now I have the time to reflect on what I experienced and saw in China while working intimately for seven years with the children of the one-child policy—their mindsets, their beliefs, their behaviors, their aspirations, and their future in a communist country that is slowly becoming more isolated and restricted in how they want to raise and prepare their youth for the future.

My former boss just told me recently via WeChat that the current Chinese government is trying to implement a national policy that focuses on making sure "our children know who they are as Chinese, and focus their education on everything that is Chinese, that they must not be exposed to or led astray by foreign ideas and new thinking. I have no choice but to follow my government at the moment. I still hope to send my son to study in the USA one day." She is confident of her plans and future for her only son.

And I said loudly, "If that is the current goal of the Chinese government, they should stop all the young people now who are leaving China, thousands of them studying all over the world. The government should stop them from learning Western thinking and beliefs and practices. They will bring back to China this new thinking and Western ideas and ideals. It is so ironic that the government is trying to prevent the youth in modern China from any exposure to Western thinking today. What about the future when these young people return to mainland China?"

I also told her, who hired me to work in her department in China, that while she assigned me to teach courses on American history and culture, current affairs, and British history and culture, I would never say to my students that the American or British system or way of thinking is better than or superior to our Chinese thinking or culture. My task then and will always be to expose the bonsai kids to the big world beyond the four walls of their country. Only through embracing the whole world as citizens of the world can we hope to establish and live in a peaceful, harmonious, and prosperous universe. Yes, every country has something unique to offer to the rest of the world. And as citizens of the world, we can continue to share our rich culture, beliefs, traditions, and practices and also to learn from each other. And together, we might be able to save this world from self-isolation and destruction. My interest in this book is to explore the one-child policy in China and my exposure to and involvement with the children of this policy during my seven years as a visiting professor in the country.

CHAPTER TWENTY-NINE

Yicheng is located in landlocked Shanxi Province. Unbeknownst to the general public in China, for over a quarter of a century or since 1985, Yicheng and several other rural counties were part of a *secret* experiment where the people could have two children regardless of gender. In some rural parts of China, they would allow couples a second child if their first was a girl. With few restrictions, people in these counties did not resort to infanticide or sex-selective abortions for unwanted daughters as most Chinese would prefer males instead of females for traditional reasons. And surprisingly, birth rates were also below national average. By all accounts, this would be considered a success in *jihua shengyu* or planned birth program. But it made no real difference to the central government.

And years later, demographers would hold up Yicheng as an example of a future China. A little known economics instructor, Liang Zhongtang, was the only critic of the one-child policy in a conference before it was launched nationwide in 1980. He warned that the policy would be a terrible disaster, leading to a society without a future. He is the man who coined the famous phrase *4:2:1*, referring to a situation where two adults would have to support four elderly parents and one child, and an aging population with little familial support. Today 4:2:1 is in everyone's vocabulary when talking about their children or bonsai kids.

In fact, in many rural areas, many children who left when they were young had abandoned their aging parents, leaving the central government to take care of them. Remember, major earthquakes in China also killed many young people before they could finish their education. And many left-behind parents are also relying on the central government for assistance. One could blame it on the one-child policy.

So who is Liang Zhongtang? He was unable to attend college in 1966, the year Chairman Mao Zedong launched the Cultural Revolution, which closed down all schools, allowing and encouraging his Red Guards to be on a decade-long war against intellectuals. So he read Marx and Engels while a soldier and eventually became an instructor at a local party cadre school. And in the late 1970s, he was asked to teach demography, which was then removed from university courses after the Cultural Revolution (1966–1976).

And so at the time when the central government launched its one-child policy in 1980, the leaders were not sure how many people there were in the country, and this shocked some scholars. But the leaders knew that China was drowning in *tai duo ren* or too many people and that China would forever be poor and hungry unless they did something about *tai duo ren*. Because of medical advances that had lowered infant mortality rates and lengthened life span, China leaped from 540 million people in 1949 to over 800 million in 1969, a span of just twenty years. Population growth was unprecedented. *Tai duo ren*.

Since the 1950s, China had been practicing population curbs through legislating early marriages and distributing condoms and IUDs. Different policy, different time. China, new in the game of population control, was learning in the process.

In the 1970s, they introduced the *wan, xi, shao* campaign, meaning "later, longer, fewer," encouraging couples to marry later, space out their childbearing, and have fewer children. Many scholars were impressed with the results of this campaign because it was a huge success in curbing the soaring population. Beijing remained unmoved. If that was so, how did the one-child policy come about?

After Chairman Mao's death in 1976, the new breed of leaders felt the decade-long *wan, xi, shao* campaign was too slow for turbocharged growth. They were more interested in improving GDP per capita quickly. Deng Xiaoping, Mao's successor, was eager to set a goal of quadrupling China's GDP per capita to one thousand by year 2000. Population planners believed China could not reach this ambitious goal with a two-child policy, so they must tighten the restriction to a one-child policy. It was an arbitrary economic goal, and by 2000, China's population had past the 1.2 billion goal, with GDP per capita more than tripling past Deng's original one thousand mark. And the central government continued to stress the need for the one-child policy.

The Communist Party Central Committee and China's leaders promised that the one-child policy would be temporary and that, in thirty years, they would adopt a different population policy if they could control the current population growth. After WWII, population numbers crept up everywhere, not just in China; people made love, not war, and babies followed around the world. Paul Ehrlich, a Stanford professor, in 1968 wrote the book *The Population Bomb*, saying that the battle to feed all humanity is over and that hundreds of millions will starve to death. And even the United Nations joined the war to curb population growth in third world countries (China included) by launching the United Nations Fund for Population Activities (UNFPA) in 1969.

While in mainland China, Song Jian—a Russian-trained ballistic missile specialist—would play a major role in China's eventual adoption of the one-child policy. How did this happen? He believed science could fix all the problems related to the results or obvious consequences of the one-child policy, like diminished workforce over time, aging, women's average fertility rate, and how to determine how many babies women in China could have. Science was the key to solving all problems, he believed, and he pursued it with a vengeance.

In 1975, Song Jian was with a Chinese delegation to the Netherlands, where he met a young Dutch mathematician who shared with him a paper on how to prevent overpopulation on a fictional island. And on returning to China, he would use this and other European scholars' research as a basis on how to control China's birth rate. His formula would clash with Liang Zhongtang's proposals at the 1979 population control symposium in Chengdu. At this meeting, different proposals on how to curb China's population were discussed. The one-child policy was not the only solution. But Song Jian's findings would soon make their way into China's mainstream media, and eventually, the one-child policy, the most extreme of all, was adopted and accepted as the only solution to China's population problems.

And so on September 25, 1980, the Communist Party published and sent an open letter to its members asking them to voluntarily limit their family size to one child, and thus began China's most contentious, most radical, and longest-running social experiment on family planning in the world. It lasted three more decades before the Chinese government announced in late 2015 a reversion to a two-child limit. The policy allowed exceptions for the fifty-five ethnic minority groups. Many critics believe the term *one-child policy* has been a misnomer because, for nearly thirty of the thirty-six years that it was implemented, about half the parents in China faced instead a two-child limit. Sadly, with this reversion from the original one-child policy, many independent women in China now refuse to march to the same tune, arguing it is too expensive to have a second child.

Without the keen support of today's independent women in China, the new policy of having more than one or two children will not work. Don't be surprised if the Beijing government has many tricks up their sleeves. This is China.

CHAPTER THIRTY

A new marriage law was launched in 1980 lowering the legal age of marriage to twenty for women and twenty-two for men. More unions meant more babies. The same year, the central government adopted the one-child policy. This applied primarily to married couples as procreation was not for those outside of marriage. That was the assumption.

What kind of world did people live in when the Chinese government implemented the one-child policy across mainland China? Imagine someone in your community or neighborhood who kept track of every household's reproductive habits and reported these details to the village's family planning commission. This information answer questions such as Are you single, married, sterilized, or pregnant? What kind of contraceptives are you using? Do you have one or two children? You could not hide any secrets from the planning commission officers in your neighborhood. You felt like someone was watching your every move in your private bedroom.

Throughout the 1990s, many women were sterilized after the birth of a second child, or births must be spaced at least five years apart. You felt like your bodies belonged to the communist government. Sex was for procreation, not for personal enjoyment.

Sichuan Province was one place where sterilization were largely done on men because it was easier, faster, and less likely to result in complications. Li Shunqiang, a doctor in the province, pioneered a surgical technique for vasectomies in 1974 called no-scalpel vasectomy, now widely used in many countries in the world. Now you know why Sichuan Province was the model for family planning. Another by-product of the one-child policy was the use of abortion by some as a form of birth control, making it difficult for some women to conceive again because of scarred tubes through multiple abortions.

Examples of one-child policy propaganda or slogans by the government are "Late marriage, late childbirth benefit both country and people" and "Fewer births, swifter prosperity." At the time, with people who grew up with memories of hunger and starvation, the idea of having fewer babies to feed was very attractive. Nevertheless, those who failed to observe the one-child policy would be hit with fines between five and ten times their annual disposable income. And what if you don't have the money to pay the fines? Many families could not afford the harassment from family planning officials; some ruthless officials might smash household things to teach them a lesson. They would remove things from your house, like bicycles, tables, and washing machines, and the proceeds from the sales would be kept by the township.

Many women were afraid of the side effects of sterilization, though China favored it because it was virtually a foolproof way of lowering your fertility. Or you could opt for barrier contraceptives or promise not to have more than two children. Some knew nonpermanent barrier methods like IUDs, the pill, and condoms were not trustworthy.

In 1983, China sterilized over twenty million people after the one-child policy was launched in 1980. In some places, pregnant women without birth permits were marched off in handcuffs to undergo forced abortions. In some places, officials ignored or paid mere lip service to the orders from the central government.

And by 1984, the one-size-fits-all one-child policy proved very unpopular, so the government introduced Document 7, allowing each province more power to adapt the policy to local circumstances. For example, people who lived in many rural areas were allowed to have a second child if their first one was not a son. And places like Yunnan and Tibet with large ethnic minorities had more liberal policies. But with Document 7, local officials had wide discretion determining how much to fine people who broke the rules, a system ripe for corruption.

The local provinces were responsible for funding the bulk of population planning on their own. It would seem that local planning officials were keen to arrest people because the more you arrest, the more bonus you could earn. And even doctors were incentivized to perform more abortions to increase their bonus. The more the sterilizations and the more the abortions, the more money coming to the local planning officials.

You could see that bribery was inevitable because of this system. Not everyone caught breaking the law was treated equally, depending on where you lived in China. And one common form of bribery then was to pay planning officials for a certificate stating the bearer was not pregnant. But the baby would pay a heavy price later because he or she would be considered an illegal human being and would not be able to get his or her *hukou*; without it, you had no life in China.

CHAPTER THIRTY-ONE

Many Chinese parents came up with all sorts of creative ways to confront the policy—fertility treatments for twins or triplets, birth tourism, fake marriages, and bribes. By the third decade, a third of the population facing the one-child policy could afford the fines for a second or third child. You could say that many, by now, could afford to break the law and pay the fines.

Most China watchers knew that the policy had irrevocably shaped the face of modern China and inevitably resulted in a host of social and economic problems that would endure for decades to come. The one-child policy tilted gender and age imbalances. Because of the one-child policy, over thirty thousand men or the "bare branches" could not find a wife in mainland China. Also, China's population is aging faster than anywhere else in the world. That is not good for China because a large graying population means a less productive country. Over the coming years, China will be losing seventy million or more of its workforce, a warning not only to China but also across the world as China is the core of the supply chain.

This is one major reason why China is moving to a consumption-driven model of growth, trying to encourage increased domestic spending and expand the service sector. Because of the one-child policy, there will be far fewer working adults to support a retiree population, thus straining China's rudimentary or nascent pension and health care systems Also, most urbanites have accepted the reality of smaller families and support it. Because of the one-child policy, an estimated thirteen million children are undocumented or *hei haizi* (black child), a term denoting children born outside the one-child policy. *Hei haizi* are children who are not registered in the national household registration system because their parents gave birth to them illegally, breaking the one-child policy. That means this child does not possess a *hukou*, which is essential for a person to access any type of government service. That means education, hospitals, travel, and even jobs are not available to *hei haizi*. And so many of *hei haizi* are forced to work on illegal jobs in organized crime, even prostitution and drug dealings.

The central government is slow to recognize that the one-child policy is rapidly imperiling future growth to create a population that is *too old, too male, and too few*. Most economists know that more people, not less, is one reason for China's boom. Many economists will agree that China's rapid economic growth has more to do with the central government's moves to encourage foreign investment and private entrepreneurship than a quota on babies or the one-child policy.

China's massive, eight-hundred-million-person workforce started to contract in 2012, and its shrinkage happened faster than anticipated, thus driving up wages and contributing to global inflationary pressures. China's vast number of workers is growing old, and by 2050, one out of every four people will be over sixty-five. The one-child policy has shrunk the working population that must support and succor this aging people. China has rolled out nationwide pension and health-care schemes but the social safety net is far from adequate.

Some economists would rank the one-child policy as one of the most obvious strategies to slow global warming, though most would admit that the real culprit was the Chinese government's "economic growth at any cost" model, which erected environmental protection measures that had a more detrimental effect on global carbon emission than the number of children born in China. China has officially moved to a two-child policy as of late 2015 to ease demographic pressures. Ironically, the one-child policy can be judged a success because many people in modern China, especially those in urban areas, have internalized the mindset that a one-child household is the ideal family. This could be the reason why many modern independent women are not keen to have another child despite the central government's reversion to the two-child policy since 2016.

CHAPTER THIRTY-TWO

I had the privilege to return to China almost every year after 2015, and I would learn and gather more information about the one-child policy by talking to former colleagues, friends, parents, and former students, now many pursuing professional careers after graduation. Over a cup of hot Chinese tea one morning, I was talking to a professor friend in his apartment in the campus in China. In this particular university, professors were offered apartments at a special discount. He bought one when the price of an apartment was affordable. In this particular university, many older professors own and live in apartments inside the campus. I am not sure if this is a common practice across mainland China.

According to him, "The one-child policy was introduced to set a limit on the number of children parents were allowed to have."

"Making it the world's most extreme kind of population planning," I said. "In most countries, family planning is about providing the right kinds of contraceptives to assist women in having the number of children they want. Not so in China. Here, it was designed to set a limit on the number of births parents could have."

He went on, "*Yitai zhengce* or the one-child policy was first introduced in 1979 but modified beginning in the mid-1980s to allow rural parents a second child if the first one was a daughter."

"That is interesting. I understand that the policy also allowed exceptions if you are one of the fifty-five ethnic minority groups in China. Correct? In fact, I was told the term *one-child policy* has been called a misnomer because, during the near-four decades of its practice, about half of all parents were allowed to have a second child," I said.

"An American like you did not know that over 90 percent of China's urban, not rural, households were subject to the one-child policy. Families, which would include many ethnic minority groups, in rural areas would need more hands to work in the farms. So what you said is true, but you must remember the rich could afford to pay the penalty for breaking the one-child policy. Anyway, that is where the term *little emperors* came from, children of wealthy urban families."

"What do you mean?"

"That means the children of this one-child policy, about one hundred million of them, will eventually shoulder the burden of having to take care of aging parents and grandparents. It is a serious social issue facing the children of this generation with limited help now available from China's still nascent social safety net." He went on, "Dubbed *xiao huangdi* or little emperors, a big question was raised whether this generation of *only children* would lead to a nation of overindulged or overpampered children."

In my research, from observations, tests, games, and studies designed to analyze the different traits of little emperors, they found some children to be complainers, whiners, self-centered, less independent, less generous, with less self-control and weaker life skills, less trusting and trustworthy, averse to high risk, more pessimistic, and some feeling unlucky and pressured.

"It is important to note that, according to economists, only 15 percent of the so-called little emperors had siblings," he said. "In a way, they got all the attention, excessive attention, from their parents and grandparents."

My students would tell me that, when they were growing up alone, they would ask their mother for a baby brother or a sister, and she would often ignore them. Some mothers would simply leave the child alone at home and went to their daily business. The door would be locked, and the child would be alone for hours. Many of my students experienced loneliness; no wonder they asked for a little brother or sister. I do know that some of my American friends would have two dogs or cats so they would have someone to play with. And children are no different.

He continued, "This generation of little emperors is the most affluent in our country and history, and they have never known anything like drought or famine or the Cultural Revolution but soaring economic growth and prosperity around them. As the only child, they get everything from their overprotective parents and grandparents."

"Very true, yet some of the children are preoccupied with a sense of living under pressure because of the excessive parental love. Some of them feel embarrassed and guilty that their parents are making huge sacrifices for them. With their own dreams crashed, especially during the ten years of the Cultural Revolution, 1966–1976, these parents hope to realize their dreams through their only child. The children feel they are walking the path their parents did not finish."

"I totally agree with you. With parental sacrifices come great parental expectations."

The young people today are faced with skyrocketing property prices. They experience China's expansion of higher education, with about seven million or more college graduates hitting the job market, resulting in high rates of unemployment. Their parents have come from a background in which lifelong employment was a guarantee.

Now they are facing growing restrictions on social mobility. In late 1990s, there was a sense that anybody could rise, provided you worked hard. Within a short period, the sense of limitless opportunity appears to be slowly diminishing.

In 2009, Peking University sociologist Lian Si coined the term *ant tribe* to describe the overworked and underpaid college graduates, especially those who came from the rural areas in China, total strangers to the major cosmopolitan cities in mainland China; and with their rural *hukou*, they were denied many social services and privileges only for those with urban *hukou*. Across China, employers were known to complain that little emperors made poor hires. Some employers preferred candidates with siblings. Why? Because single children were quick to complain about the difficulty of the job and would quit.

Diaosi, a name associated with the little emperors, is a term for the male genitalia that is a slang for losers, someone who takes an ironic pride in their lack of prospects. Because of its popularity, the Communist Party of China put an immediate stop to it.

In 2012, a Renmin University academic, Du Benfeng, coined the term *one-child family risk*, warning that any accident suffered by a member could mean a disaster for the whole family. And this fragility is exacerbated by the tendency of one single child to marry another single child.

Children of one-child policy come under great pressure to sacrifice migration, career opportunities, and job mobility and some even marriages to someone from a different province to please their parents. Remember how bonsai kids were raised in China, the by-product of strict parental design and control. With parental sacrifices come great parental expectations.

CHAPTER THIRTY-THREE

And now the obvious question is why the one-child policy lasted so long. Or why did it take so long before a group of academics and reformers would use the tools of logic and research to undo the one-child policy? In 2000, an ad hoc group of top demographers with former officials tried to show that the one-child policy no longer served China's purposes economically or socially. It was time to end it as it approached its third decade. They turned to the secret two-child experiments advocated by Liang Zhongtang. Faced with the social costs of a lopsided gender balance and an aging population and armed with evidence showing that China's fertility had plunged to below replacement rates, the reform group in 2004 declared that it was time to loosen the one-child policy. But the central government was not convinced.

In 2006, the reformers went to Jiangsu Province, where they tried the *dandu* policy; *dandu* refers to couples in which one spouse is an only child, but only a tenth took advantage of the freedom to have a second child. In 2008, the reformers went to the government with updated findings. Eventually, they took the debate publicly and shared their findings and thinking to the nation's top news media. They sought the help of economists on the effect of the one-child policy on the labor markets. James Liang—founder and CEO of Ctrip, China's biggest online travel site, who holds a PhD in economics from Stanford and wrote *Too Many People in China*—argued that the one-child policy would quench entrepreneurism and innovation.

After more than a decade of behind-closed-door lobbying, the reformers sent an open letter to the National People's Congress, "the highest organ of state power and the national legislature of the People's Republic of China," arguing that urgent changes needed to be made to the one-child policy. Finally, Beijing announced in 2013 that it would fold the Population and Family Planning Commission into the Ministry of Health, a critical step in the slow phasing out of the one-child policy.

Eventually, some demographers came around to Liang Zhongtang's way of thinking and called him a hero and a national treasure. Year after year, he was unable to persuade the central government to adopt his two-child proposal nationwide. The question now is, will all childbearing women support the new two-child policy to meet China's aging population and labor shortage?

CHAPTER THIRTY-FOUR

The post-1980s generation of sibling-less children, the bonsai kids, growing up as an overcoddled and pampered only child without siblings to interact with, is accused of serious personality traits: being selfish, incapable or unwilling to compromise, apathetic to the needs of others, extremely impulsive, less trusting and trustworthy, averse to high risks, more pessimistic, self-centered, less independent, less generous, having less self-control, and having weak life skills. They are the complainers and whiners, and some feel unlucky and pressured.

During my seven years as an American visiting professor in mainland China, I had the privilege of knowing many students, and somehow I failed to detect their many negative personality traits. Maybe I was too busy teaching them and ignored all the nonacademic facets or aspects of the students I was with daily during my seven long years in China. Maybe the academic world is the wrong place to study the personality traits of the bonsai kids directly under my supervision. Maybe college students are a different breed from those bonsai kids who are less privileged to pursue a college degree. Maybe the hoi polloi of China is intrinsically different from the college crowd.

When I first decided to write this book about bonsai kids, I immediately contacted many of my colleagues, friends, and former students in mainland China to seek their opinions, reactions, and input. Almost all of those who willingly and happily wrote and shared their stories did not major in English in college, and I am truly impressed and inspired by their ability to write their stories in English. They could have written them in Chinese and later translated into English.

As a visiting professor in China, I was impressed with many of the Chinese students and their eager pursuit of foreign languages. I did not and do not sense that in students in the United States of America. I know of mainland Chinese students who pursued advanced studies in Korea, Japan, Germany, Canada, England, Russia, India, Australia, France, Italy, Spain, and the USA. Just recently, I was talking to a Chinese student in China who told me he wanted to pursue his undergraduate degree somewhere in Germany. He had just finished his Gaokao and was now ready to embark on a new chapter of his life, going to college—but not in China.

"Germany?" I was curious. "I didn't know you know the German language."

"No, I do not know any German, but I started taking German classes now after high school. And I should be ready for studies in Germany this coming fall," he said confidently.

In my mind, I knew he would succeed in his new endeavor.

CHAPTER THIRTY-FIVE

Here are the incredible voices of some of the bonsai kids who are happy to share their stories with all of you. Each person is unique, and from them, you will learn that each is different from the other. I will not define them as selfish, uncaring, inconsiderate, indifferent, or averse to opportunities or challenges as each tries to make the best of what is available or given to them. Nevertheless, all of them strive to make the best of their lives, grateful to their hardworking parents who have raised them the best they know how despite the different circumstances in their lives. If anything, all share one thing in common: they are all children of the one-child policy in mainland China. I hope the stories will touch your life as they have deeply touched mine.

PART ONE:
FROM CHINA TO AUSTRALIA
by Jay Qi-Long Han

My name is Jay Han. I was born in Changde, a peaceful city in Hunan Province, China. I was born in 1995, and because I was a second child in the family, my parents were made to pay a fine to the government because of the one-child policy. That meant my parents had broken a law in the country.

My brother is three years older than me. I was lucky to live with my parents and grandparents, and we were a busy, happy family. My grandpa would always take me on his rusty green tricycle to my primary school. He was a hardworking farmer. He would always take me to school no matter how bad the weather was. Grandpa was a warmhearted and optimistic kind of man.

My parents encouraged me to study hard and urged my brother and me to study tenor saxophone when I was ten years old. It cost my parents about fifty Chinese yuan for a forty-five-minute lesson when it only cost three yuan for my daily breakfast. The music lesson was tough and boring when I had to practice by myself. But I did pass level four in tenor sax in the end. I also learned how to sing and had both tenacity and perseverance in what I did. I could sing well when my friends and I would go to a karaoke bar. I also learned to play the guitar and had my own songs too. Music has become a very important part of my soul and life.

PRIMARY SCHOOL

I was not a good student in primary school. After our classes on Fridays, my friends and I would visit the illegal internet café to play computer games and eat some junk food. During summers, I would go with my brother and friends to swim in the Yuan River, which is near our house.

Overall, I have an unforgettable memory of my primary school. Yes, I was young, naive, simple, and innocent. I will miss the time in spring when my friends and I played games on our school playground. I will miss the time in the summer afternoons when we broke nap time rules to play electronic games. I will miss the time in autumn when we climbed the trees to pick fruits after school. Yes, I will miss the time in winter when I received good grades from school and shared them with my parents, sitting in front of a wood fire and waiting for a reward for my hard work in school.

MIDDLE SCHOOL

As time went by, I finished primary school with good grades. Then I started another journey.

I felt lucky to meet my English teacher, Cherry, who had visited the USA such as Hawaii, New York City, and so on. She was a nice teacher because she often showed us a lot of pictures of the USA, which impressed me, and from then on, I was curious about foreign culture and the world outside Changde. I missed the US coins as a reward for good performance as a student. I missed every single Christmas Day when she threw a party during the class and celebrated it with a tasty big cake. And that was how she planted my love for English, and it grew in my heart.

I felt lucky to meet my good classmates too. Amazon and Thomas were my best middle school friends. We experienced many things together: swimming across the Yuan River, playing basketball together day and night, and also traveling. Yes, we laughed, we sang, we hugged one another. I learned to treat them like brothers.

I was also a gambler. There were a lot of "tiger machines" in small "7/24 shops" near my house that attracted my attention. Every day when my classmates went to school with books inside their backpacks, I went to school with a few coins. Something bad happened after I became addicted to gambling. I stole money from my parents. I was caught in my crime. My mom punished me with a big stick, but I continued the bad habit.

I also gambled playing the cards. I was also addicted to it, and one time I lost all my money to my high school classmates. Good memory was essential to winning the game, and I did not have it. After I lost it to my friends, I approached my brother, hoping he would help, but he refused and rejected me. That was the end of my gambling with cards. That was the end of my gambling.

HIGH SCHOOL

I knew I did well in my middle school because I got the opportunity to study at No. 1 High School in Changde, my dream school. The school is over a hundred years old.

There was a foreign teacher, named Stan, who came from the USA. Stan was tall and had a girlfriend, Linda, who was also from the USA. She taught in another city near my hometown. At that time, my English was too poor to understand him. I should have asked him if he knew Michael Jordan. Instead, I used the Chinese pronunciation *Qiaodan* (Jordan in Chinese), and he was confused hearing it.

I think I was a daredevil because I was not afraid to talk to a foreigner even though I could not speak English well. I felt very cool about it, and I was dreaming of going abroad in the future.

TKK COLLEGE

The reason I chose Xiamen University Tan Kah Kee (TKK) College was that I loved the coastal city of Xiamen, which is famous for its romantic and artistic vibe. Besides, I always wondered when I was young if I could live in a place close to the ocean; then I could go fishing or go to the beach, and that would be a lot more enjoyable. After I arrived at the campus, I knew I was right; my campus was not only modern and big but also lovely, like a painting. I miss the summer when the phoenix trees blossomed, and the graduates took photos of their happy faces. I miss the foggy mornings when the whole campus was just like paradise. I also miss the tasty food from the three student canteens and snacks from outside the campus.

There are quite a few memories about my four-year college life. First, every summer holiday, I had one and a half months of free time. Instead of going home directly by plane, I preferred to detour on my way home. For example, I used the one thousand Chinese yuan to travel around Shenzhen, Zhuhai, and Canton by train and eat local snacks and stay in hostels. Likewise, I traveled to Zhangjiajie and Fenghuang. At that time, I realized that I loved traveling and enjoyed talking to different people I met on these trips.

Second, when I was in TKK, my major was computer science and technology. I loved math, which made me think things logically. I loved English, which brought me to get to know more interesting people and places. Gradually, I felt like I was not good at dealing with computers, and so I changed my major to tourism management. And this was a hard but correct decision in my life because if I did not change my major, I would not be going to Australia.

Third, I loved English, so I took part in an English club called Ensanity. And Steve Ling, a visiting American professor, was very involved with it. I was lucky to know him. We met weekly at the Ensanity club meeting. He told me he was impressed with my fluent English and my confidence to speak in front of other students. When he told me he would be happy to work with my English, I was lucky to have him as my personal mentor. I learned many things from Steve, but most important was his advice and encouragement to spend a gap year in Australia. Both Australia and New Zealand had initiated a program for young college students in China to come spend a gap year in their country. And I took that opportunity to go to Australia to work and also to improve my English.

So when Steve mentioned that I could go abroad, I was excited but also afraid. I desired to go abroad because I had this thought since I was young when I saw the photos from Cherry, my middle school English teacher, and also in high school when I talked to Stan. However, I was still afraid with doubts and questions. Would I be eligible? Could I pass the IELTS? Would I have enough money to travel abroad? What if I could not find a job or face some discrimination over there?

At that time, Steve was very patient, and he reached out his students who were in other countries to tell me how life was in a foreign environment. Besides, he had confidence that I should not have any problem with IELTS. With Steve's encouragement, I started to prepare for the IELTS in the summer of 2015. The next step was to persuade my parents. After I shared my ideas with them, they did not hesitate; instead, they supported me in following my heart.

Where there is a will, there is a way. Luckily, I passed the IELTS; and after a long wait, I finally got my work and holiday visa (WHV) to Australia. That's such an unbelievable experience in my life. And I had decided to defer the last year in TKK College and did the gap year in Australia.

GAP YEAR IN AUSTRALIA

First two months in Sydney

On October 24, 2016, I flew from Changsha City to Sydney with curiosity and excitement. I chose that day because October 24 also can be written as "1024," which is a good number in computer science and technology. You know, 1,024 megabytes equal 1 gigabyte of data. At that time, I only had one thousand Australian dollars with me, one luggage, one backpack, and nothing to lose, right?

I went to find my friend Angelia, who came to Australia five months earlier than me. And she introduced a "cash in hand" job to me after two weeks without any job offers. If she did not do it, I might be homeless in the end. While I was in Sydney, I never stopped trying to find a legal job. After two months living in Sydney, I finally received two offers; the first one was a casual tour guide in Sydney. The second one was a full-time job as a housekeeper on Hamilton Island. Hamilton Island, in the tropical Whitsundays, is Australia's favorite holiday island destination. Staff or islanders would call it "Hamo." I decided to go to Hamo because some experienced backpackers told me it was a lot easier to save money in the regional areas compared with metropolitan cities. Financial independence was the thing that I was looking for.

Heading to Hamilton Island

On December 20, 2016, I flew from Sydney to Hamilton Island and started an unforgettable journey. Hamilton Island Enterprise (HIE) had more than one thousand staff, and most of the frontline positions were given to temporary visa holders, like students with WHV. Many of the staff workers were from all over the world: Africa, Europe, Asia, North America, South America, and also the Pacific islands. What an opportunity to get to know the different cultures from around the world!

Jobs

I held more than ten positions during my gap years, such as salesman, worker, cook, housekeeper, waiter, kitchen hand, houseman, minibar man, and tour guide. And one of my favorites was public area (PA) cleaner. I called myself a Great Barrier Reef (GBR) caretaker. It was true that the PA cleaner, which belonged to the housekeeping department, was literally a caretaker of the environment in GBR. My daily job was not that hard but needed to follow the SOP, making sure all the public areas were clean and tidy.

During one sunrise, I saw two wallabies eating grass on the oval; and when I finished my job, I just lay down on the couch and drank beers. What surprised me was that my salary was ten times higher than while I worked as a receptionist in a Sheraton Hotel in China. Everything was better here in Australia, and if I worked for HIE for a year, I would get a one-month annual leave with 20 percent more payment. What a paradise! And this dramatic change happened within four months. Life in Hamo was promising and enjoyable for me.

Free time

In summer nights, when I finished my work, I preferred to grab an XXXX Gold beer and went fishing at the airport jetty, with the Milky Way and shooting stars in the sky and a breeze rippling the surface of the sea under the moonlight. I was living my life.

One night I caught thirty-two squids. At that time, it was the first time my friend Vinnie came with me to fish. And he felt that it was too easy and was bored of catching a fish. But that was the biggest night for me, and I could not resist the temptation when there was a group of squids wandering around my lure.

Farewell or birthday parties are great opportunities for people to mingle in Hamo. Everyone would bring one food or drink to the party to share, such as handmade sushi, BBQ, pizza, and other specialties. When we finished the meal, we would dance, talk loudly, or sing songs.

I also did a road trip along the eastern coast during my annual leave. I and my friend Sharming, with two Taiwanese friends, started from Airlie Beach, and we drove the motor home, following the Bruce Highway to Brisbane, Sydney, and Melbourne. That was my very first road trip; we spent the night in the car, stayed at a farm, saw the bright stars with dogs barking, and stayed at the beachfront with a view of the beautiful ocean.

Hard time: Cyclone Debbie

It was around March 2017. Cyclone Debbie, the strongest tropical cyclone that hit Hamo since 2015, uprooted trees and caused serious damages to many homes. One night while working a night shift, a heavy rain flooded the backyard of the hotel, with water entering the housekeeping area, lobby, and concierge. And the roof was damaged by the strong wind. The following days, we had no lights, internet, even water. I was scared, but it was exciting.

Ex-girlfriend

Hamilton Island is a honeymoon island, so it is perfect if you have a loved one here to enjoy the sunset at One Tree Hill with a cocktail. I had one; her name was Jenny, who came from Malaysia. Jenny was one year younger than me, and she had a Chinese background. Although she was young, she had studied in Melbourne for more than ten years, which was impressive to me. I was lucky to have this girl while I was in Hamo. We would spend the night after work for the day and then had dinner together. On the weekend, we hung out at Airlie Beach, which is the closest mainland town. We were eating good food and staying in a bungalow on a heavy rainy day. All good things must end, and we broke up.

Overall, during those twenty-two months in Australia, I did skydiving, had road trips around the East Coast of Australia, met many people from around the world, tried different jobs, and earned more than one hundred thousand Australia dollars.

Stay in Australia or not?

Basically, I was thinking that after my work and holiday visa expired, I could continue to study in Australia because I had roughly forty thousand Australian dollars to support me, but that meant I would give up my bachelor's degree in China because I still had one more year to finish my studies. However, Steve wished and encouraged me to go back to TKK to finish my last year if I wanted to. I can get the bachelor's degree and then return to Australia. I was faced with a dilemma. Without too much hesitation, I decided to take Steve's advice, which was more rational and reasonable.

Back to Australia to study

After I went back to China to finish my last year, I had three options: apply a work and holiday visa to New Zealand, continue to work at the hotel, or study in Australia. I decided to try to work in a hotel first. After I successfully worked as a team leader in Sheraton Hotel for three months, I was keen to go back to Australia to study. Because pay in China was too low to afford my daily life, I lived with two coworkers with no privacy, and it was hard to enjoy my life, always working overtime without any pay. Most importantly, staff's turnover rate was too high, so most of the frontline workers did not have enthusiasm.

Meanwhile, I got a five-thousand-Australian-dollar scholarship from the university that I applied to. I then managed to persuade my parents to support me. I was lucky because my parents said yes to me because they did not want to let me down.

Now I am studying for a master's degree at the Blue Mountains International Hotel Management School in Australia. In the words of Steve, "Do what you have to do to get to where you want to be."

PART TWO:
THE JOURNEY TO MEDICAL SCHOOL
By Michael Qiao Jia

My Chinese name is Qiao Jia, and my English name is Michael. I was born in 1994 in a rural family in Shaanxi Province, considered a poor area in mainland China. My father works in a coal mine. My mother helps raise four children. Her health is not good.

I grew up in a poor family in rural China. Life was difficult. Children from rich families could afford everything, like things they needed for schooling, and they had the money to enjoy their summer and winter holidays.

For us children, we paid a lot of attention to our schooling. We loved learning. We could not afford to have all the materials to do our homework. But we studied hard.

My father did something very special for us children. He gave us a sheep so we could take it up the mountain after school so the sheep could enjoy the grass up there. We were innocent children, and we made the best of what we had. We climbed trees and played sandbags and hide-and-seek. We were too young to understand the importance of education. I will always remember the red scarf we wore, the symbol of the Young Pioneers.

My parents attached great importance to my education and arranged for me to go to a primary school in a town not far away from home. The first English word I learned was *blackboard*. Of course, we heard a lot about the 2008 Beijing Olympic Games. Unfortunately, we also heard about the Wenchuan earthquake in Sichuan Province that killed many students. I was in junior high school at the time.

I studied very hard because I wanted to become a doctor. I wanted to help my mother because she is not a healthy person. I was able to enter Chongqing Three Gorges Medical College. I wanted a better future for myself and my family. I worked very hard for the computer qualification certificate, CET4, and the National Medical English Grade Certificate. I won many awards and was ranked seventh in the overall medical performance in a class of more than seventy students.

And while in college, I was lucky to do part-time jobs as a tutor and sales clerk at Juran Home and Haier and also did some heavy manual work. After I graduated in 2018, I worked in a community health service center and took part in a civil service exam. I failed the civil service exams not once but three times and finally passed the test. I am happy to be a civil servant, working for the country and my government.

Poverty did not stop me from working hard and achieving my dream. I knew the importance of learning and working hard to be who I am today. I believe I could change my fate, and I did and continue to improve my learning and life.

I would like to thank my American friend and mentor Steve Ling. I was lucky to know him when I was in high school. Steve always encourages me to do my best. I will always be grateful to him for being my mentor, who is always there when I need his voice and advice.

Now I must work hard to enter graduate school to become an effective doctor in my life. What a life! Poverty did not stop me from becoming a doctor, and I will continue to improve my life and career through working hard and continuing to improve my knowledge in the medical profession.

PART THREE:
FROM HUAIHUA, HUNAN PROVINCE,
TO SEATTLE, WASHINGTON STATE, USA
by Duan Xi

I was born in a small city named Huaihua, located in the middle of south China. Just like most families in China, my parents anticipated and invested a lot in my early education. I had been taking different kinds of classes like penmanship, mathematics, and sketching besides normal schooling since my primary school. My teachers were most proud of me, and I was able to attend one of the best junior middle schools as a result.

However, I changed a lot since I joined the middle school. I became addicted to computer games. I played computer games all the time if I was home alone. I even tried to get up in the middle of the night to play computer games after my parents went to bed. They also tried hard to prevent me from playing it, like taking away the cable, mouse, or keyboard and always checking if the computer was hot when they returned home. My dad even caught me twice when I was playing in the night. However, I was always able to find a way and continued playing. But I still did okay in terms of grades at the time because I had a good foundation since my primary school. Besides, I was able to focus on my studies. And I really enjoyed solving some difficult mathematical problems in class. I just did not spend any extra time in my studies.

I would go to an internet bar with friends since I started playing more player-versus-player (PvP) games, and I spent thousands of yuan for playing there. Besides, to play for just twenty minutes after school, I had to go to an internet bar that was close to my house. Sadly, my dad was working on the third floor while I was playing computer games on the first floor in the same building.

Even though I played a lot, I made it to the best high school in my city, and I was even able to pass the exam and join the best class. (Our high school has sixteen classes in total at the time, and only two of them are the best, equipped with the best teachers.) In the class, most of the students studied really hard, but I was still able to find a couple of friends who shared the same interest with me. We played basketball after school and computer games whenever we got a chance. So my grade was always a little bit below average, but during the last year of high school, I studied harder just because I did not want to fall behind.

I had no idea about what I was going to do in the future. I had no target and did not know what I was studying for. I just did not want to get a lower grade than others. Sometimes I really enjoyed solving a difficult mathematical problem that others could not. I proved I was better than others. But I had no plan for the future. During the last mock exam before the college entrance exam, my grade was in the top thirty among all the students.

However, the college entrance exam was a big setback for me. I was too focused on solving hard questions and did not pay much attention to easier ones. So I made a lot of stupid mistakes. As a result, I was only ranked 150, which was way worse than I expected. I felt so upset during the whole summer and was determined to make a change.

So college became a new start for me, and computer games became less important. I spent more time doing new and useful things. I joined the student union, became the leader in my class, and organized all kinds of activities. I spent lots of time in the library and did some research projects with teachers. I was always thinking about how to improve myself. So during my junior year, I had received many honors and got the top rank among the students in my major for three straight years and was awarded the top scholarship.

I decided to do something even more daring—study abroad. I had several considerations for that: (1) I want to make use of what I had achieved, like good grades, some projects, leadership, and so on; (2) I don't want to take the risk of taking another master's entrance exam; (3) I really want to see the world out there.

And I chose the United States of America as my destination. I was accepted for a master's program in transportation engineering at Virginia Tech. I took four classes in my semester, which was extremely intense, and language was one of the main problems for me. When the teacher asked questions in class, I hesitated to answer as I was not sure if I understood the questions correctly, even though I knew the answers.

During the first week of class, when the teacher asked all students to team up to discuss some questions, nobody wanted me in their group. But everything changed after the first homework. When people knew I was the only one who was able to solve a problem, everyone came to me and asked me to explain to them how I did it after class. Even though I was terrible at explaining things in English (especially when you need to explain a mathematical question), all of them were patient and were listening to me carefully.

I joined the professor's lab during the first summer, and I published my first paper, which was an extended research from one of my classes I took that time. I also found a part-time job during the summer at our university's bookstore, which sold mainly electrical stuff like computer, iPads, headphones, and so on. It was challenging to me, especially trying to answer phone calls on orders. It was almost impossible for me to write down the names and addresses. I sweated all the time. Luckily, people around me were supernice and helped me a lot. It was a chance to practice my English.

During my second year at Virginia Tech, I mostly worked on my second paper, and I made a decision to pursue a PhD. Since my professor did not have enough projects to fund me, I had a chance to pick a topic for my second paper. I chose a topic that was totally different from my first paper and my professor research area because I wanted to do something new. I stayed in the lab all the time and worked really hard to finish the paper in time. My professor was superhappy about my work and wrote a very strong recommendation letter for me. Because of the research topic of my second paper and also the recommendation letter from my professor, I received an offer from a professor from the University of Florida (UF). (I did not want to stay at Virginia Tech because a tech school does not have many girls.)

After I moved to the UF, I made the decision to focus more on preparing for a job and less on doing research. I started taking different classes in other departments: statistics, computer science, and industrial engineering. It was extremely intense as I needed to attend classes and finish the research work my adviser assigned to me at the same time. Sometimes I would skip a class and just learn by reading the textbook to make better use of my time. (I skipped all the classes during my last two years at UF.) But I almost got all As for the courses I took.

During my second year, I wanted to quit my PhD as I wanted to work in the computer science area instead of transportation. Why? First, I was passionate about building products. Second, I could earn more as a software engineer than as a transportation engineer. So I talked to my adviser, and she agreed and continued to fund me as I would keep working on her projects. I started looking for software engineer and data analyst jobs at the same time. It was extremely difficult for me to find a software engineer job as most of the companies were seeking students with a computer science major. But I was lucky to get an interview with Amazon and passed it.

I was initially assigned to the Nashville office when I got my job offer, but I received an email from the director of the organization asking me if wanted to join the office in Bellevue, Washington State. I was excited because I have many friends in Washington State. So I drove all the way from Florida to my new job in Washington State in the Pacific Northwest.

To me, the key to success is one's ability and willingness to adapt to new possibilities in life and also to do what you have to do to get where you want to go, even if that meant giving up my PhD in transportation engineering and pursuing a new dream, leading me to Amazon in Seattle, Washington State.

What a journey for me, from Hunan Province, China, to Washington State, USA.

PART FOUR:
FROM XIAMEN UNIVERSITY, CHINA,
TO BROWN UNIVERSITY, USA
by Chao Chen

I grew up in a small rural town in the inland region of Fujian Province. Located about fifty kilometers away from the world-famous Wuyi Mountain National Park, this small town has its fair share of beautiful terrain. Hundreds of miles of mountains with evergreen forest stretch to the end of the sky.

My parents had been living in this town their whole life. In fact, the farthest they traveled was to the Wuyi Mountains for their honeymoon. The idea of leaving this town had never occurred to them. It was probably because they knew so little of the outside world, and few of their family and friends had ever left. It would be beyond their wildest dream that, one day, their son would travel across the Pacific Ocean to pursue his dream in a country thousands of miles away.

Generations on my father's side had been farmers, so being a farmer was a natural thing to do for my father. He started working in a farm soon after he turned fourteen. He was the eldest son in the family, so he had to share the responsibility of raising his younger brothers and sisters with my grandparents. He worked hard in the farm so he could help my grandparents bring enough food to feed the family.

My mother was born in a relatively well-off family. My grandparents on my mother's side owned a breakfast café. Although having enough food was never an issue to the family, my mother's childhood was not easy either. She had to wake up at three in the morning every day to help her parents in the café, making buns and cooking porridge.

My father and my mother got married when they were twenty-two and twenty years old, respectively. I once asked my mother why she was willing to give up her relatively comfortable life and marry my father, who was a poor farmer from a poor family at that time. She told me that she knew my father was a hardworking, good guy, and she believed that they would be able to build a happy life together through hard work. As soon as she married my father, she started working in the farm with him. My maternal grandmother told me that she cried numerous times after she saw the condition of the farm and the tough work her daughter had to do every day. But she said that she respected her daughter's choice.

My parents had always been hardworking as long as I could remember. They left home for the farm early in the morning after sunrise and came home late in the evening just before sunset. When they were not at home, they asked my paternal grandmother to take care of me. Occasionally, when my grandmother was not available, they took me to the farm and kept an eye on me when they were working. Those were the happiest days in my childhood because I did not have to go to school and was able to run freely in the farm and chase all sorts of small animals. However, observing how they were working in the farm was an important experience in my childhood. The image of them working in the farm would later become a source of strength to overcome the challenges in my life.

[I have written extensively about Chen Chao's incredible upbringing and schooling in my two previous books: *This Is China* and *Letter to Fellow Immigrants: A Memoir*. Though he signed up for his undergraduate study in economics when he enrolled at Xiamen University in China, the university assigned him to study computer science. He further pursued his master's degree in computer science at Brown University, one of the top Ivy League schools in the USA. When he finished his master's degree in computer science, he consulted his parents—both farmers growing vegetables in China to earn a living—about studying economics at Brown because it had some of the top professors in the field in America. It was at this time when Chen Chao talked to me, expressing his profound sadness and regrets that he would have to return to China; maybe it wasn't in his destiny. Maybe it wasn't meant to be.

It was at this time that I told him to pursue his dream to study economics and that I would be happy to support his dream. He did enroll to pursue his first love to study economics at Xiamen University but denied that privilege. Brown knew Chen Chao would be a beginner in his new academic endeavor in economics and required him to finance his first year, and if he did well, Brown would finance his PhD in economics till his completion of his studies. I wanted Chen Chao to achieve his dream, but I could only do so much financially initially, and he and I decided he should take a year or so off to make some money to continue his studies. He did, and it was at this time that I suggested that maybe he should return to Xiamen University and that, with his academic achievements thus far, he should have no problem securing a scholarship to study economics at Xiamen. He said simply to me, "Steve, Brown has the best economics department in America. Why would I want to return to Xiamen for my PhD?" I understood his determination to study at Brown. He left the campus and worked, hoping to save enough money to continue his studies at Brown.

I was a visiting professor in China when Chen Chao wrote me an email dated March 20, 2012.)

> March 2012
> Dear Steve,
>
> I hope this email can find you well before your birthday, 31st March. Hope you had or will have a lovely birthday with your beloved students.
>
> As the spring break starts, I finally have some time to sit down in a quiet corner of the library and think about the questions in my mind for a long time. I would like to thank you again for what you have done for me. Chinese people believe that everyone gets

lucky in his "own" year. I was born in 1988, which was the Chinese year of the Dragon.

So my own year is the year of the Dragon. 2012 is the year of the Dragon. I think I have been very lucky this year. I started to study economics at Brown with your generous financial support. I have been influenced by the world-class economists at Brown, whose knowledge, personality and attitude towards life have been enlightening me.

I am enjoying my life here, a simple, busy and rewarding life. I am learning from the great minds in the world and I hope some day I can become one of them and do as what they are doing for the people and the world.

I'm grateful for the gift of your friendships. (Message of this card.)

My life is changing towards a bright direction of which I could hardly dream before. I am grateful for your help, with which I can fully pursue my passion in economics and pursue a happy and meaningful life. Happiness is shared, just as you said. I hope someday I could do the same thing for others just like what you are doing for me.

Thank you and happy birthday!

Love you,
Chao Chen

Brown University
Providence, Rhode Island, USA
March 19, 2013
Dear Steve,

Thank you for being there for me and supporting me in my life. I wish you the best of blessings and good luck on your Happy Birthday!

Dear Steve, this is your 5th year in China. You have devoted your life, passion and love to helping students. I wish to thank you for everything you have done for me and every smile you have given me. You are one of the few who have believed in me every step of the way. You are one of the few who truly understand my dream. You are one of the few who I always think of in the face of difficulty.

Dear Steve, it is my privilege to know you and share laughter and tears with you. Thank you for being a friend who is always there when I need you. Thank you for being like a father to me and a beacon of light when I lost my way.

Dear Steve, all the times I have spent with you are going to be sweet memories for the rest of my life.

Happy Birthday!

May the Lord bless you!

Love you always,
Chao Chen

September 12, 2021
Dear Steve,

I cannot believe it has been almost 10 years since I wrote the March 2010 letter to you. How time flies! I completed my PhD in economics at Brown University in February 2021, exactly 9 years since I enrolled in my first introductory course in economics. I still remember that 9 years ago after I told you about my passion for economics, you said those words to me: one course per semester and you can do it. I did exactly what you told me to do. One course per semester. Now I have a PhD in economics. Sometimes a humble beginning may seem too little or too late to make a big difference. However, with determination and perseverance, one can still achieve a great deal. My life so far has been a testament to that.

I started my job as an economist at Amazon in Seattle, USA in March 2021. I got married recently and I will become a father later this year. My wife is an architect in Vancouver, Canada which is just about 2-hour drive from Seattle. I plan to buy a house along the US-Canada border so my wife and I could commute to our work places in a reasonable time. I also would like to invite my parents to live with us. They have sacrificed so much for their only son. Now is the time for them to get some rest and enjoy their life.

I am so grateful for everything I have right now. If you told me 10 years ago, I would not have believed it. I am grateful for having met you in my life. Your encouragement and friendship have helped me go through challenging times in my life in the USA.

Love you,
Chen Chao

PART FIVE:
SEVERAL STORIES OF MY LIFE
By Minwei Ai

Part One

I stood near the small eggplant land, seeing off Mama, who was walking down to the river slowly. A bag was on her back. She was going to a remote place. It would cost several days by bus and train. I didn't know where it was. Mama didn't turn back. She was crying.

Days ago, she had a quarrel with Papa. Then the sulking started in our family. They didn't talk to each other. Now Mama decided to leave temporarily and emotionally, maybe for several years.

That seldom happened between them. After their marriage, after the birth of a son and a daughter, they managed to have a better life. They worked very hard on the land. But it was still not enough to fill mouths.

In the first several years after my pa and ma got married, Ma always laid sick. There was a story told by Ma that can illustrate how hard their life had been. Pa once went downtown to buy medicine for her. At the final step to pay, he checked out all his pockets, yet he couldn't find another five bucks, only five. In the street, Pa saw a person he knew. He ran to him to borrow and was told he had no money.

His life lay in bed. It seemed it would never come to an end. The young husband became scared. There was nothing he could do. Ma could hear his sighs and sobs. Pa was afraid to lose her.

It was true. Pa was frightened to lose her because he had lost his ma and pa. Grandma left him when he was a baby in the cradle several months after birth. And on his sixteenth birthday, Grandpa passed away too. Papa was the youngest child of my grandparents.

When Papa got a wife and had a son and a daughter, he tried his best to pull them together, to give them hope. But now he can't make it. I saw Mama leaving for money, which the young family had long suffered from.

Ma boarded on a ferry. I saw her. Something was stealing my heart piece by piece, until all was empty. She went off the boat and was climbing a hill farther and farther. Finally, I lost her in my eyes.

I stood there. My aunt said, "Now you don't have a mom."

"None of your business!" I struck back.

"Dead kid!" she returned.

At the moment, tears flooded out of my eyes.

Part Two

For the aunt who made me cry, I didn't hate her at all. She is my big uncle's wife and lived next to us. At lunchtime or suppertime, I often went to her table and had a check with my bowl. She taught me too. Papa was not home sometimes, and I had to cook for myself. I always asked her to slice the potatoes for me as I can't use a knife. She did it for me. And when I was cooking, she would stand aside to tell me how much salt, soy, or gourmet powder to put in.

Another time I would like to spend with her was to look for fodders for pigs in the wild. In the small mountainous village, every family raised their own pigs. Most were for sale, which was the main income for villagers. And one or two would be butchered at the end of year for the spring festival. In my house, there're often two in the pigsty, one for the tuition of my sister and me and the other for meat for the next year.

Only in spring and early summer were there not enough fodders for these beasts because crops were still green in the field. So collecting wild vegetables for pigs became a daily job for housewives. I was glad to do that to help Papa. It was every afternoon after the sun faded. I would take a small moon-shaped knife and a big basket. Sometimes we looked over in the bamboo groves. Sometimes we moved in the deep wheat and corn land. I got to know plenty of herbs from my auntie. I may not have some of their names, but I know which are poisonous and which are eatable by animals but fatal for human beings.

Sometimes in the fields, if lucky, I might have a glance at rabbits. Once, I saw one, and it flashed by me. Of course, snakes were disgusting and horrible. They may give you a terrible bite. And in my auntie's philosophy, encountering snakes, especially a two-headed one, was a bad omen. That's why I am prejudiced against snakes.

Often, I was earlier than auntie in filling the basket because she was far less flexible. Every time we moved to a new spot, I acted quickly and cut all that was tender and green. She was aged then and can't bend down for a long time. Auntie always complained to me, but she was never angry.

When bound for home at dusk, the basket was so heavy for me to carry. Sometimes Papa would pick me up, or auntie helped me.

Part Three

In the east end of Sichuan, down deep mountains runs a branch of Yangtze named Daning (peaceful) River, where my father once fished. Papa owned a little wooden boat with a bamboo roof, a bed in the middle, and a cabin at each end to store fish and cookers. My younger uncle would often join the journey when the boat went to fish far away. And several times, they took me.

Where they fished was in a deep mountain gorge sandwiched by high mountains, I could truly feel how remote the sun was from me. In the afternoon, they put nets down the river or set hooks with baits beneath the rocks, which was the most important part of fishing. Pa squatted on the deck to do this, and my uncle sat at another end of the boat to control the rudder. Most times, I was kept in the middle. But I still remember some exceptions. I sat beside my uncle, and he picked up some floating apples for me with a net.

In the gorges, monkeys haunted in the trees or on the cliff. When they appeared, Father or Uncle would say, "Wow, grandsons there!" I'm not clear why they had to say that, just hearing some stories. Monkeys pushed rocks down and sometimes shot the boats or people below.

There's not much kerosene to burn decades before. So we went to bed very early every night in the gorges. But you can seldom fall asleep immediately. After daytime, animals started to enjoy their time. Wild goats came down to the riverside to drink flock by flock. Owls hooted in the woods. And there were also some other voices that you cannot identify from animals or otherwise. Sometimes I felt some things were moving near our boat; even their steps can be counted clearly. It made me feel cold, and I had to hide all my body under the blanket that reeked of smoke. "They dare not get on our boat as hooks and nets are hanging," Pa said.

A new day of fishing always started with a busy early morning. Papa had to pull up and check all the nets and hooks. Some big fish can take the hook away. So then we had to look for it by a floating bottle. Often, catfish and giant salamander gave my father and uncle lots of surprises and smiles, which sold high even it was illegal. Big fish was for sale, while small ones were for bait and our dish. Pa would also say "damn it!" when a crab got on the net because it might leave a big hole on it. For me, the only joy on the narrow boat was watching fishes swimming in the cabin that was connected with running water by several small holes.

Meanwhile, there's a saying from Pa. If he saw a man grazing his buffalo when setting out to fish, he may get a big catfish in the journey. If a woman holding a baby, he may hunt a giant salamander. Then it was all up to luck.

At noon, all nets must be cleared, washed, and hung in the sunshine. After that, we cooked lunch on the bank. A darkly iron pot was hung above the fire. Burned firewood was abandoned on rocks by floods. Clean water came from the springs or waterfalls. We had steamed rice, fresh fish, salted turnip slices, and jam sauce but no green vegetables. The spot where a stream ran down from the high mountains, groves of bamboos thrived, and three or so wide, flat rocks lay was a perfect kitchen. In rainy days, we had to find a cave instead. Staying in it, watching rain dropping, it easily induced my homesickness.

If rain continued, Papa also began to worry about how to go back home, for too much rain threatened a heavy flood. And at the other end of the gorges, Mama would climb up to the hilltop to watch the way back home. Sometimes it was me standing on the hilltop, watching and praying, praying and watching.

Part Four

I removed the soil, and then a broken plastic bag came out. I took away the cover. Now I saw the hay. Beneath it, small sticks lay there one by one. Another layer of grass followed. Finally, my eyes caught the real things in the little hole, still golden and fresh. Thank god they got through the long chilly winter safely.

Last autumn, when frost started to fall, I was busy with choosing an appropriate construction site. It must be a place of highland to let water go easily and rich in soft soil, which allowed me to dig deeper. Apart from those, it better be away from the other kids. The farther, the safer. If it was below a tree, that would be very good natural shelter, and I can remember its location much more easily.

In fact, there was really such a site where there were a big tree and few stones, and the soil was mixed with sand. So I started my work. First, I drew a circle on the ground and dug out all the soil inside. All I used were a short stick and a stone as big as my fist.

The wood was not so large. It was used to grow shallots and garlic before my birth. Perhaps just after the first harvest, the land got rested and was left to wild grass and trees I seldom knew about. But for a child in the countryside, this wasteland was a paradise. I shared the happiness with birds, ants, crickets, and other unknown insects. When I can't find any ant upside or beneath rocks, I knew the winter was coming. And winter would be gone if I heard the robins singing again.

Now I got to the bottom of the hole and saw thick tree roots. Digging was over. Then I picked up the stone "hammer" to punch the wall, making it more solid. For the bottom, I had to lay a thin layer of small stones from the wet.

It was time for the treasures. De jure, they were not my treasures. The only work I did was to make them look like mine. They were oranges and tangerines, fresh ones. In my hometown, a valley in the Three Georges of Yangtze River, the mountainous land was comfortable cradles for oranges and tangerines instead of crops. In late autumn, these fruits turned into golden yellow gradually. It was delicious, but we can't eat all of them. The common method was to keep the rest fruits in a cellar. If you left them on the tree, they would all be killed by the chill.

I managed to make it like that. And the wall was solid enough after plenty of punches. The dried grass was already prepared, like the warm blanket of fruits. Then I stood up and went to the fruits hanging on trees. Most trees belonged to my two uncles. Perhaps they didn't mind so much letting me have some stealthily. I sheared them off one after another, and I left several pieces of leaves with the fruit on purpose. I put them carefully in my arms.

Returning to the hole, I arranged them in the dried grass. Then I placed the sticks and plastic paper, namely, the roof of the hole. It came to an end. I covered the hole in the soil I dug out before. I punched it hard and set some fallen leaves upside. I looked at it now. Nobody, except me, would know that there was something hidden underground.

They were my secrets. Just in the wood, under the ground, I buried them with my childhood memories.

Part Five

I may not sit here and have a university life if Papa didn't go to school to talk to the head teacher in my grade three. I may be a peasant now, working on the little land or a migrant worker hanging about in a city that I don't belong to. The last two years of primary I passed lazily and carelessly. In class, I never listened to teachers talking and played crazily after class. At home, I just did a bit of homework to pretend that I did do it. So you can imagine how my score looked like, always more or less 70 percent.

And one time, the worst came at last. I didn't pass a mathematics test. Papa was called into school. I was sitting in the classroom. My classmates called me from the other side of the window. "Hey, your father comes!" They laughed and then crowded at the gate of the teacher's office. I buried my head in my arms.

I can't remember what Papa had said with the teacher or with me. But it did sort of hurt me. In other words, it awakened me, making me feel shameful about myself, giving me the need to earn respect from my teacher, from classmates. Since that day, I started to change myself into a good student. De facto, I made it. It turned out that I have the ability to reach it and gave me more courage and confidence to fly higher and higher. This is the first turning point in my life, I think.

Papa also gave me much help. He would teach me how to work out the math exercises every afternoon. And later, I can all handle by myself. My formative education came from my parents. One morning Mama was making fire to boil sweet potatoes and green vegetables for pigs; the flames were out and wood crackling. Papa picked out a piece of charcoal and wrote a math equation on the wooden back door. They asked me to give the right answers. Of course, I can use my fingers. Mama was watching.

However, I didn't do them neither wrong or no answer. Papa said I would not be allowed to have lunch if I can't make it. It was the earliest education I knew from my parents. Although I was scared to lose lunch that time, I can understand it was the couple's hope and expectation on their son, their love. They wanted their son to be different from them, getting away from the land and the small mountainous village. They gave me dream, and I'd fulfill it.

Another time, it was rainy in the morning. My sister was stuck on the way to school. She didn't go to school anymore but returned home with her bag. Papa asked her to go to school. And she just didn't want to go. My sister was asked to do farmwork, collecting vegetables for pigs. I just knew from other people that she really did it. However, she went to school the next morning. And now she went to study in a university.

Part Six

The Three Gorges Dam began to store water in 2003. A new town was rebuilt at the top of a hill near my home. Ships to the county and the town stopped at the riverside down the hill. Suddenly, the riverside was full of people.

My parents found business there. They set up a shed by the riverside, planting four pillars, circling bamboo fences, adding asbestos tiles as roof. That was it. The door was a roll of plastic.

Papa had been fishing all year round, while my mama had been farming every day. They never did business before. But they decided to "cross the river by feeling the stones." At first, only cigarettes and instant noodles were sold. Later, snacks and drinks were added, and a freezer was bought. They learned to keep accounts on a crumpled and oiled notebook. Names, quantities, and prices of various goods, as well as the mobile phone numbers of different people, were recorded on it "not seriously." I always found many wrong spellings. Nobody can fully understand it except my parents. Mama had not finished elementary school, while Papa dropped out from junior high school.

At the end of each month, Papa and Mama would sit on the bed, carefully adding and subtracting the income and expenditure according to the accounts book and then counting each cent in their hands. Mama also learned to do market analysis. For example, if something was selling well this month, then more of it would be stocked the next month.

Several weeks after opening, Papa placed a fence inside the shed. Then we had two rooms. The larger one was a living room, filled with tables, chairs, and benches. Passengers can sit there while waiting for their ships or friends. They can also play cards while they were waiting. The smaller one was used as a kitchen. Mama moved in coal stoves, pots, pans, bowls, and plates. Their little restaurant opened, selling noodles and wonton.

I was then in junior high school but ate and slept at home. Since they started the business in the shed, our kitchen moved there too.

However, I was truly not used to having lunch under the eyes of many strangers. I was raised in a mountainous village where few strangers came and villagers seldom went out.

For the first time, I would rather starve in the old house than eat in the shed. Mama and Papa called my name again and again from the riverside. I just did not want to go. Finally, my papa climbed up the hill, walking home with a full bowl of hot wontons in his hands. He said, "Eat, or it will become cold soon."

Papa still went to fish every afternoon. The fish caught were kept in a cabin in the river. River fish was always popular. If passengers were willing to eat, Papa cooked for them. Many liked the taste. The secret was my mama's bean sauce. Papa prepared fish soup for my lunch. I didn't like it. It was fishy. In his view, fish soup was good for me because studying was brain consuming. But I refused them. "The fish will not make me smarter because you caught the stupid one."

Papa had a wooden boat armed with two paddles. Each time he went to fish in the gorges, Papa had to paddle for almost two hours. When a speedboat was passing by, the small boat would shake up and down. It seemed to be eaten by the waves the next second. Papa knew how to handle it. He made the boat cross the waves obliquely. When the angle was forty-five degrees, the turbulence would be very small. Of course, if the driver in the speedboat knew my papa, they would slow down.

Gusts of wind and rain often hit the summer afternoons in the mountains. The sky was getting darker and darker, the rain began to hit the hot ground, and my papa's boat did not appear at the exit of the gorges. Before he went out to fish, the boat was usually unloaded as far as possible to make it move fast. He did not bring a raincoat. Papa must be wet.

The rain poured, crackling on the asbestos tiles. Boom-bang-boom-bang! Worst of all, the wind was blowing. To prevent the roof from being lifted, Mama hurriedly fixed the fence and tarpaulin, and my sister and I also came to help.

The heavy rain shot from the gloomy sky to the river like thousands of arrows, and winds strengthened the waves. The whole river instantly became boiling. Still, we did not see my papa's boat; mama was panicking. She grabbed an umbrella and ran along the riverside, standing at a point of the bank, staring at the surging waters.

Finally, there was a boat. Winds and waves were too strong to paddle in a straight line. Papa had to move the boat to the riverside and proceeded meter by meter. He shook the oars vigorously in the gray rains and high waves. He was soaking wet but stood. His boat kept on being filled with rains and waves. When he finally arrived, the foam and bottles were floating in the boat. Water dropped from Papa's hair and coat.

Months passed. Another shed was set up down the river, and ships migrated there. My parents' business was not doing as well as before. At that time, I had already gone to high school in the county, and I went home only during long vacations. There was a holiday in the middle of a semester. When I got home by ship, it was already dark. The water had risen to 165 meters. Our shed site was flooded, and things were moved to a new place.

In the darkness, dim lights leaked out through the fences. I walked in. Piles of stuff scattered on the ground. Papa and Mama were there, bending over, sorting things silently. I called out, "Papa!" They immediately turned back. After seconds, smiles flooded their faces.

Part Seven

Papa walked me to my high school. In the junior graduation examinations, my grade was not good enough to get an offer from the schools in Chongqing. Although I received the enrollment notification from the best school of our county, Papa still worried a lot if I would be selected into the best class.

There already gathered many parents and students in the campus when we reached it. Lawn, red and white buildings, and plastic playground—these all were so far away from me before. I left to watch the luggage, and Papa went to fill out all kinds of papers. A while later, he and I were led to the dorm. It was a long journey; all steps led up to a hilltop. As the bed lacked a mattress, Papa headed back to the student supermarket and bought some thick boxes. He took them apart, pressed them flat, and set them under my bamboo mat. When all was finished, Papa had to leave. I saw him off at the enrolling site.

He asked me to give them a call if any was demanded, and he would come and bring me a thick quilt when the autumn fell. I nodded. I saw him slowly pushing through the crowd, and he turned back several times. He wore a dark brown shirt. I still stood there. Then he turned a corner and got out of my sight. My heart was empty at that moment. It was the first time he left me in a totally strange place. Many years passed, and I still remember his number and the situation; he walked by a corner and disappeared from my eyes.

His phone number was 13996502676. I used the commercial telephone in the supermarket to call him or Ma every week. Once, my papa answered my call; he was out of the house and chatting with someone. I asked about Mama. He ran back home, climbing the steps. I heard it. He was as happy as a kid. "Our son called!"

In the second year of high school, I dialed my pa's number one afternoon. He was in a hospital in Chongqing. I asked him when he would come back. There was no response. I waited and repeated. Still no response. I thought it was a sign of a problem. But it was not. It turned out to be his last conversation with me.

Part Eight

After Gaokao, I went to visit my grandma. She lived in a small village high in the mountain where my mama grew up. In September, I would go to a college far away in the east coast of China.

The path stretched in the mountains. From my village to Grandma's, it was a two-hour walk. This was the first time I walked alone. When Papa married Mama, he walked. When my mama returned home with kids, she walked.

Wild grass bred on the path. Farmlands were abandoned. Houses were there, but doors were locked. Residents migrated into cities, working in factories in the coast. Most of them never returned. Villages in the high mountains were left to trees, grasses, and wild animals.

In a valley, huge white flowers were opening to the sun. They were wild lilies. Some grew in stone pits or beside thorny bushes. I never saw them before. At this time, the holly flowers were blooming enthusiastically under the sun. In Chinese traditional weddings, white lilies are often given as a gift to the bride and bridegroom, meaning that they will love each other and stay together for one hundred years.

When I arrived at my grandma's house, she burst into tears when I mentioned my father's death. Uncle was silent. In those years, he turned older suddenly. It is said that a nephew will look like his mother's brothers. We kind of looked like each other. At least we had almost the same number of moles on our faces.

My uncle showed their paddy field to me. Rice was hanging in the husks, and the leaves were light yellow. On the ditch, we saw a blooming lily. I hurried home, fetched a hoe, and planned to dig out the bulb. Uncle said he would do it for me. He took the hoe and dug deep to take out the little bulb. It should be such a wonderful thing for people to stay together for a hundred years.

On the way back, my uncle picked a handful of bitter vegetables and prepared them for a hot pot at night. My aunt cooked bacon in the pot. Uncle smiled bitterly and told me there was no fresh meat at home. The bitter vegetables were planted to feed pigs. When rolled in the greasy pot, they turned delicious. My uncle was getting older, and there was almost no income from farming. It was not so easy.

Before leaving, I asked my uncle to dig some peltate yams for me. Although they tasted bitter, Mama and I loved the taste. Grandma told me she survived the famine by eating yams. As a Chinese medicine, the government advocated the planting of the yams. Farmers responded, but no one came to buy them.

Yams planted on the slope was thin and old. Uncle tried several sites. All were thin. I said that these were enough. But he insisted to dig in the ditch. It was wet, and yams grew large. He was right. Although poor, my uncle wanted to give me what he had.

I took the lily and yams. Grandma, Uncle, and Aunt saw me leaving under an electronic pole at the top of a hill. He still said little. Grandma was sobbing. I walked all the way forward, not looking back. When I was a kid, Grandma would stand under the pole and see my four-member family leaving each time after spring festival visit. She boiled eggs and put them in my pockets.

Back home, I planted the lily bulb in a pot. Hope it would sprout in the next spring, grow, and bloom.

Part Nine

"You're such a foodie," my roommate Xiao Lai said to me before.

Actually, I was not a real foodie, but I do not deny that I am very positive about eating. During military training, our commanding officer pointed out, "If you are not active toward eating, there is a problem with your life attitude." Everyone laughed at that time. In this sense, my life attitude was active, at least for the four years in college.

When it's time to eat (eleven o'clock for lunch, five o'clock for supper), "Eat! Eat! Do you want to eat? Who is going to eat?" I yelled. "Xiao Lai, are you going? Play with your computer after eating! Shi An, are you going?" After such a call, the two roommates would slowly close their computers, take the student card, and go to the cafeteria with me. We three were often together.

After graduation, Xiao Lai found a job in Xiamen and rented a room outside. I was going to study my postgraduate in the same college. On the day of leaving, while packing his luggage, he said, "After moving out, I won't hear your calling, 'Xiao Lai! Xiao Lai! Let's eat!'" When these words flew into in my ears, I was a little sad.

I never had a real friend in the first twenty years of my life. I was raised in a mountainous village where people lived far away from one another. In high school, I (or we) was busy with learning and countless homework. I had never lived in a dorm with three peers for four whole years. But in college, I did many things together with my roommates. Another roommate—Shi An—would go to Shenzhen. Although he looked very manly, he cried so hard at the gate of the university before entering a taxi.

In Xiamen, for a few years, I couldn't get used to the fried lotus root slices in the cafeteria. It was too sour. I guessed too much vinegar was put in. I didn't like fried oyster at first. It was too fishy. I, however, fell in love with it later. Another food, no matter what kind of fat, I don't eat it.

Once, I had supper with Shi An in a canteen. I ordered twice-cooked pork. Most of it was fat. I bit the skin and left the fat. Shi An finished, eating fast. His plate was clean. He put his head in his arms, stared at me, and said disdainfully, "If you are my brother, you must be beaten. You left so much meat."

The same thing happened after one or two years in another canteen. Shi An did not eat the fat. I immediately told the story to him. He smiled and asked, "Did I say it?"

I firmly believe that my memory is correct. Many things that happened in the past, and my head can pack them one by one and store them in different drawers. The earliest impression of eating was the memory of a taste. I was in the second year of elementary school. After school, I walked home with a small umbrella. It was more than forty minutes. White fog wandered on the path and hillsides. Autumn rain dropped, hit my umbrella, and then dripped down. Occasionally, a drop of rain fell on my face, making my body tremble. I couldn't remember whether it was too cold or I was too hungry.

When I got home, my schoolbag was almost soaked. But as soon as I stepped into the house, I smelled a special aroma. It was not Mama's cooking. It was dry and crunchy and had a hint of sweetness. I even felt that it was leaking out from the bedroom. As I ran to it, I asked my mama what it was. Wow! A big bag of popcorn, tightly tied. It was even warm. How happy I was. Even now, when I open the drawer of the memory, the wonderful flavor overflowed again.

I told Mama the story. She said she had forgotten it. She, however, remembered another story that had been forgotten by me. I was very young. My big uncle was frying meatballs. He gave me one and asked me if I wanted another one. Mama immediately said "no, thanks" for me. Turning a corner, I murmured, "Mama, why did you say no? Actually, I want one more."

Part Ten

Many people asked me why I study journalism. It is difficult for me to explain it clearly. Anyway, the result is that I am now studying news. Put simply, this question can also be asked in another way. "Why did you choose the major of journalism after Gaokao?"

Da Wei—the one who sat next to me for three years in high school—and I went together to an internet bar to apply to universities and majors after Gaokao. At that time, Mama, my sister, and I were living in a small dim room outside our high school. In fact, at the beginning, I did not choose journalism. My first choice was accounting. My history teacher suggested me that I choose it. Other choices included finance, international trade, and economics. Obviously, all my favored majors were related to money. I was thinking about learning something to make a lot of money. (This dream has not come true yet.)

In the internet bar, my friend told me that a relative of his family worked as a reporter in Chongqing and had a good income. I hurriedly checked the majors of Xiamen University. There was journalism. So I added it to the end of the long list.

Of course, I was not admitted to accounting or economics. In September 2008, I went to college to study journalism. There was a meeting organized for all the students from Chongqing. We stood on the basketball court and chatted in the Sichuan dialect. One asked me, "Where do you come from in Chongqing municipality?"

"Wushan," I replied.

"Where is it?" He was curious.

"In easternmost Chongqing," I explained.

It seemed that he didn't know where Wushan was. My county is located in the mountains, far away from the central district of

Chongqing municipality. In that meeting, I also saw the guy who studied accounting. I decided not to say a word to him because I would study it if he did not. Since then, I had never participated in these meetings.

Although my selection of majors seemed not serious, I still had a lot of connections with journalism. In May 1999, when the old Chinese scholar trees in our elementary school just had new leaves, I was a third-year student. During the break, a group of students surrounded a corner of the playground, making noises. At the forefront stood Mr. Ma, who was writing something on the blackboard. I didn't understand what he wrote, but I heard the words *Yugoslavia*, *embassy*, *US*, and *bomb* from the mouths of senior students.

In fact, Mr. Ma was not designing a poster. He was copying a student's article. That student was older than me, in sixth grade, and he lived on a hillside by the ferry. Later, I heard that the senior student watched the news that our embassy in Yugoslavia was bombed by NATO from CCTV. He thus wrote down his feelings and submitted it as homework to his teacher. Mr. Ma liked it very much and wrote it with chalk on the wall of our little elementary school.

At that time, most of the people in our small mountainous village did not have TV, radio, or newspaper, and many of them had not even been to downtown in the county. When I was standing on the playground and saw the noisy and crowded people in front of me, I actually didn't understand where the place called Yugoslavia was or what happened. But I did have a dream—I also wanted my article written on a wall and read by many people.

Getting used to college life was not easy. The first lesson was to send an email. I was required to send an email to join a student association and to apply for a student grant. I was using the computer in the classroom after class and exploring how to send out an email. Another student came in and stood aside. It seemed he wanted to use the computer too. He was waiting. And I then heard, "You don't know how to send an email? Where do you come from?" My face turned red, and I felt so sad about myself. My journalism teacher—Mr. Ling—finally taught me how to send an email. He is a Chinese American and taught us English for two years.

The second lesson was how to ride a bike. In my dorm, the other three mates bought their bikes. Bike was not expensive, but I couldn't ride it. I never had a bike before. Before class started, I would leave the dorm much earlier than my mates because I had to walk. One classmate concluded, "There are two who cannot ride a bike among the boys. You are one." I would never forget how Mr. Ling taught me to ride, holding his bike, running along. Those were such happy and bitter times.

In college, sometimes you had to find something by yourself. One of my favorite courses then was Introduction to Mass Communication Research Methodology by Ms. Li. Other students might find the course boring, but I was particularly interested in it. When Ms. Li explained the operationalization of abstract concepts, she used my homework. Although she didn't mention my name, I was always proud of it. I believed that I found something I wanted to focus on.

Now looking back, I don't know how I came along nor how I will go in the future. But I think it's good to keep an active attitude. I went to teach in a college in Guangzhou after finishing my postgraduate program. And three years later, I successfully applied for the PhD program of the Chinese University of Hong Kong. This is where I am.

If I can sing, I want to sing this song to you when you finish reading these stories, my dear readers.

> Looking back on how it was in years gone by
> And the good times that I had
> Makes today seem rather sweet (not sad).

So much has changed;
It was songs of love that I'd sing to then,
And I memorize each word.
Those old melodies
Still sound so good to me
As they melt the years away;
Every sha-la-la-la
Every wo-o-wo-o
Still shines every day.

PART SIX:
I ENJOY MY INDEPENDENCE AS THE ONLY CHILD OF MY PARENTS IN MAINLAND CHINA
by Ryan Jiaxin Shen

I was born in the second biggest island in Fujian Province, China, called Dongshan Island. I am the only child in my family. The one-child policy was strictly enforced in China when I was born back in the 1990s. I did not grow up in an affluent family. My parents worked hard and gradually built up their small business from nothing. Since I was the first grandchild to both paternal and maternal grandparents, I was spoiled by my grandparents. I was so lucky to be surrounded by so much love growing up.

My dad was a long-haul truck driver. I barely saw him at home when I was little as he had been working outside. I can clearly remember a time when I attended a performance in my primary school. When it finished, I saw that many fellow children had both their dad and mom picking them up. I got picked up by only my mom. I still remember that feeling of frustration and disappointment not seeing my dad there for me. Then my father quitted his truck driving and started running a wholesale business with my mom. Now he had more time to spend with me. My father was also very strict with me about everything.

My father was always responsible for my studies, while my mom tried also to raise me. My father only finished junior high school, and my mom dropped out after primary school. In my memory, my dad could still tutor me with homework in primary school. Despite their lack of education, my parents were good parents, raising me using their experiences to educate me about the importance of education and good behavior. Like the majority of other Chinese parents, their education was traditional and conventional. They would discipline me if I misbehaved or did something wrong.

Even though my father only had a primary school education, compared with other parents, his thinking was pretty advanced and farsighted. For example, my father believes deeply that education can positively shape or change a person's life. So he would invest in my education every step of the way and would send me to a private high school and later to a private university. The tuition at this private university was ten times higher than that of a public university in China. And now I am studying here in Australia for a master's degree. My parents have made many sacrifices so I could have a good life and a better future that they did not have. They made and continue to make very challenging and difficult decisions for me, their only son.

My father prepared me well before I entered the university. Like all Chinese parents, they believed that Gaokao, the national college entrance examination, is of paramount importance to me. And they devoted their attention to make sure I was prepared for this milestone in my life. At the same time, my father insisted that children should also learn to be independent at an early age.

When I was five or six years old, my father asked me if I dared to walk to the kindergarten alone, and I said yes. When I did, he would follow me sneakily to ensure my safety. When I showed up in the entrance of the kindergarten, my teachers were all shocked and warned my parents that I should always be accompanied and supervised by adults on the way to the kindergarten.

And by the time I was ready to enter high school, my parents made the sacrifice to send me to a private school away from my hometown to a nearby city, Zhangzhou. They wanted me to have a better education and learn to be independent by living in the school dormitory away from the comforts of home.

My father would encourage children, especially boys, to broaden their horizon when they are young. He urged me to go hitchhiking, work during the holidays, and travel using my bicycle during my holidays when I was an undergraduate student. Of course, my mom would disagree with my father, thinking these experiences were too dangerous for me. Most times, I loved to travel alone, and that was troubling for many parents in my hometown.

I was born in southeastern China along the coast, where people are more traditional and conventional than many other places in China. Many parents in my hometown would prefer their children to live with them while growing up and would not encourage them to be independent at an early age. And definitely, they would not allow their children to experience the world in a risky way.

Honestly, my early independence and travels when I was an undergraduate student allowed me not only to develop independence physically and mentally but also to see the world for my myself. And these travel experiences also deepened my faith to go abroad to study in the future. Actually, although my mom sometimes disagrees with my decisions, when it comes to education, she always respects my dad's opinion.

I remember something about the strict one-child policy. My auntie (my dad's younger sister) was pregnant again. She had a twenty-year-old son, same as my age. Every day there would be some officials from the family planning department visiting my auntie and persuading her to abort the child. Yet my auntie insisted on keeping the child. Eventually, she was fined roughly fifty thousand renminbi.

Many Western people do not understand this policy, and the Western media slam the Chinese one-child policy as against humanity and being brutal. However, they just simply ignored the fact that, at the time of the population boom in China, the country was less developed, and the government could not allocate all resources fairly and effectively. Most of the areas and people were actually living under poverty. There were many considerations involved in this policy, and simply concluding this policy as antihumanity is just superficial.

With the development in China in recent decades, China has become the world's manufacturing factory and is able to provide more jobs to people. However, the government now also faces a new social issue, aging. Since many young people in China cannot afford the increasing housing prices in many major cities, they are unwilling to have babies because they do not have the money to raise them. The government is concerned about this in addition to trying to take care of the aging population in the coming decades. That is why the government decided to do away with the one-child policy and now encourages a two-children family, one way to deal with the serious labor shortage now.

Since I was the only child in my family, I admit that I enjoy all the best resources in my family. My parents are always willing to give all what they have to me. Imagine if I had a sister or a brother; I might not have gone to a private high school or TKK College or studying abroad in Australia. This is the advantage for those only child from a middle-class family. This type of family can pour all their resources and attention to one child and make sure they have the best growing up.

However, people always say, "Do not put all the eggs in one basket." If the only child in a family gets to an accident, that will be a devastating blow to any family. Also, some people would argue that raising one child in a family is not good for a child's development as they are easily spoiled by their parents and families, which might lead them to selfishness, hedonism, nonindependence, and inability to deal with hardships. To be honest, I do confront some aspects of these problems while growing up as the only child. However, since my father insisted on training me to be independent when I was a child, along with his educational philosophy of never ever spoiling a child, I am lucky to grow up almost a normal child.

Most of the time, I realize that I might be more independent than those of my age. For example, I am almost used to living alone outside my family, and I do not like to go home as often as my Chinese friends. When I was in my undergraduate school, although it was only a half-an-hour drive from my university to my hometown, I seldom went home during the summer or winter holiday. Same for now in Australia. I have not been back to China for more than three years. I have spent my fourth Chinese Lunar New Year in Australia alone, which is unbelievable for me as I have never lived without my family during the new year. If you ask me if I miss home, I would say that, well, at the beginning, I obviously felt homesick, but now I enjoy my life in Australia.

No matter where I live or work, I will always love my parents, who have given the best education anyone could ask for. And education is my key to a good and happy life.

PART SEVEN:
WE ARE LIKE THE LONELY DUSTS ON EARTH, LIKE THE STARS IN HEAVEN
By Shouheng Deng

My name is Shouheng Deng, and I grew up in the province of Guizhou, located in south China. Many domestic and foreign tourists love Guizhou because it is a beautiful place. It is definitely a very popular tourist destination for many foreigners living and working in China.

I live in this vast karst area with lush forests and mountainous peaks and caves. There are countless streams and rivers, and there is the same blue sky as the rest of the world.

To a naughty child, the weather in Guizhou freely switched from rain to sunshine. And I saw the beautiful rainbow as a child. In my primary school textbooks, I learned that the right amount of rain could nourish the trees and also irrigate the land.

Like many foreign tourists, I, too, love Guizhou because our summer is not hot, and winter is not cold. The advantage is that it saves electricity and does not need a lot of heating. So Guizhou does not have air pollution caused by boilers in winter like some big cities in the north.

However, due to this karst landscape, Guizhou has some problems related to modernization in transportation and construction. A good example is the high cost of high-speed railway construction. This problem also hinders some local plans and goals that could have been realized in Guizhou. So each project is different and requires a different approach.

I am the only child in my family. And it is true that my parents raised me like a bonsai tree with care and a great deal of love for me. My parents encouraged me to learn Chinese, math, English, physics, chemistry, biology, politics, history, geography, vocal music, guitar, broadcasting, and hosting. They also taught me how to think for myself. Both my parents spent a lot time on me and on my education. When I am arrogant, they teach me humility. When I am down, they encourage me. When I am lonely, they are always there for me. They teach me to stand up for myself if I am bullied.

Generally speaking, they are like the gardeners who keep pruning and nurturing me to be the best bonsai kid in their hands. Do my parents manipulate me to be their favorite bonsai kid, like a careful gardener trying to produce the best-looking bonsai tree? Yes and no because, most times, I do not do what they tell me to do. It is true that, most times, my parents and I will sit down together in these family meetings, helping me sort out my choices. I am lucky because my parents are teachers. And they have raised a good bonsai kid, someone with a good personality since childhood. While it is true that many children of a one-child family are known to be selfish, my parents, as teachers, taught me how to tolerate others and get along with others. I also learned how to be alone with myself, using the time to improve my guitar playing and to play basketball, jog, and sing.

When I was twelve years old, I got my first pet dog, an Alaskan malamute. Her name was Dudu. She was with me throughout my adolescence. When I would come home to visit my parents from college, I could tell Dudu missed me. I would take her out for my jogging up a mountain behind our apartment. I could tell Dudu love the outdoors. She loved spending time with me. When I sang or played my guitar, Dudu would be very quiet, like she was listening to my music. Unfortunately, Dudu died during my final year in college. I will always miss my Dudu.

For me, since I was a child, my parents taught me to be modest and polite. I might be selfish, but I always believe in sharing. I like to be kind and generous to my friends, especially my roommates in college. I am easy to get along with when I was in college. I made many friends in college because I was lucky to host many big events both inside and outside the campus because of my broadcasting background.

I am also lucky to have wonderful grandparents. My paternal grandpa, when he was alive, would teach me calligraphy because he devoted his life producing many works of calligraphy. His pieces could be seen in many places in his hometown. He always encouraged me to do my best in everything I did. He died when I was finishing college.

My mother, a schoolteacher, loves to travel. And we traveled as far as Thailand. And that is why I love geography in high school. She would expose me to many places across China. She wants me to know the world. And that is why I am hoping to further my graduate studies in the USA.

Growing up, I was occasionally asked, "Are you lonely?" It's a hot topic, but it's really fine with me. Most times, I am with people I like, and so I do not really know what real loneliness is. I think of a lonely person as someone who has no one to calm them down when they are angry and no one to laugh with when they are happy or down. I like to be busy and alone, and so I do not fully understand what loneliness is.

A lot of the movies I've seen are all about finding a partner to live with, having a bunch of friends that you can fool around and act like a jerk with, and learning to share with the people you love and care about. I am lucky because I have all these. Am I still lonely? Am I catching the current post-'90s depression trend?

No. I'm a bonsai kid, and I don't want to hurt myself. I don't want to hurt my family. I have come to this world, and I am pursuing a dream one step at a time. There is an old saying in China: "Take things as they come." I am very lucky to be my parents' only child in

China. No matter what kind of world you find yourself in, just adapt to it as much as you can. If you want to change the rules, you must first have strength. As a weak person, you should adapt well and not violate the rules.

After graduation from Guizhou University, my broadcasting professor invited me to teach broadcasting to some high school students. My dream is to build parks in the world for people to enjoy. Real happiness is shared happiness.

The world is changing fast. We must all go with the flow. I am proud to be a bonsai kid.

PART EIGHT:
HOW I BECAME AN ENGLISH TEACHER
By Aaron Sun Min

I was born in Zhangzhou, a city in the southeast Fujian Province, China. Just like many other kids born in the 1990s, as the only child in the family, I grew up living with my grandparents—either from my father's side or from my mother's side. Yes, I seldom saw my mother because she was busy working, making money; and as far as I can remember, I almost never saw my father, and I didn't know why.

Who is my father? Where is he? Why is he not here? These were the questions I had in mind ever since I was a kid, and when I asked my mother and my grandparents, they didn't answer directly. They just said he was in another city, also busy making money.

If my memory still serves me right, my father did come back to visit us a few times; and every time he returned home, I was very excited because he would buy me a lot of toys. I mean, if I saw something I liked, he never hesitated to buy it for me. But he would only stay for a few days and left Zhangzhou. This was before I went to junior school, and after that, he never showed up. I did not bother to ask why he disappeared. Even though I missed him very much, deep inside my heart, I understand there must be some reasons why he did not (or could not) come back; and yes, I always regarded myself as someone who did not have a father. Even though I didn't live with my parents, I never felt inferior to other kids. Growing up, I was a happy boy because my grandparents cared for me, and they gave me almost everything I needed—food, clothes, pocket money, toys, and love.

When I was a fifth grader in primary school, my mom sent me to a language school to study English. The school was called Sunflower, and it was located in a local university campus. That was when I began my journey to truly pursue English learning. Although I had no idea why I learned this language, I had so much fun there—learning through playing. We learned the English alphabet, basic vocabulary, pronunciation, grammar, and so on. I was not the most hardworking student there, but I certainly learned something. I realized this part of learning gave me the edge over other students when I went to junior school. I was able to do well in the English subject—quizzes, homework, exams—and I was among the top students in the class. Yes, I was always one of the best students in English all the way to high school, thanks to outstanding teachers we had at school; and yes, I continued going to the Sunflower on weekends until I graduated from high school and went to university.

Because English was my best subject at school, I decided to study English as my major in university, despite my mom's advice to study accounting—as an accountant, she thought that accounting is a promising major that would land me a stable career in the future. Honestly speaking, I did not do well in the Gaokao. With my grade, I could not go to first-tier universities in China, so I ended up going to Xiamen University Tan Kah Lee College, a private university in Longhai, about an hour drive from home. But never would I realize that this would completely change my life.

In my freshman year, I took a class called English Study Skill, taught by Stephen Ling, a visiting professor from Xiamen University, who turned out to be not just my English teacher but also my mentor. When I was a sophomore, I took part in the English speech contest at my school; and by the time I graduated, I had participated in the English speech contest on a provincial and national level, and I remember every time Steve would work with me on polishing my drafts and revising my language. He would share with me a lot of ideas and experiences, which truly inspired me. He also gave me a lot of confidence on the stage. Thanks to him, I was able to do well in the contests.

One event I remember vividly happened in my first year. Steve tried to take me to the USA for a summer holiday, and we went to get a visa in Guangzhou. Unfortunately, I failed the interview and was rejected because, from what I learned later, what I said during the interview made the interviewer suspect that I might not return to China. However, in the next year, when there was a summer camp of university students from across China, I got my tourist visa, and Steve sent me to visit the USA. In the eleven-day journey, we went to San Francisco, Los Angeles, and Las Vegas. We went to visit some famous university campuses like University of California, Los Angeles and University of California, Berkeley and had a glimpse of what the university life was like, and we also visited some famous scenic spots there. Returning from the camp, I felt satisfied. I thought, *Those are the cities that I would enjoy living, and those are the schools that I like to study at one day.*

But I believe one of the greatest inspirations I got from Steve was his passion in teaching. In the class, he was always passionate in motivating us to learn, and his classes were always dynamic and one of the few where I did not get bored or felt sleepy. Because I was inspired by him and because I had worked with him and other teachers in the English speech contests, in my junior year, I realized that if you want to be a good English teacher, being excellent in English is not enough; you have to know how to teach it. And because I had always been passionate in English, I decided to pursue my career as an English teacher.

When I shared this idea with Steve, he was more than excited. He told me that maybe I could study overseas to get a master's degree in education so that I could to not only continue polish my English but also and most importantly learn how to teach English in a way that's different from the traditional grammar translation method adopted by many English teachers here in China. This sounded like a wonderful idea, but how about the tuition fees and the living cost? Coming from a single-parent family, the tuition fees of studying at TKK were always a huge burden for my mother; I could not imagine how much it would cost to study overseas. But Steve told me that he would take care of me as long as I managed to get myself admitted by an American university.

So I started to work very hard to improve my GPA and study for the TOEFL. Because I did not have a lot of access to exam tips at the time, I decided to try TOEFL classes in Xiamen City. Going there was not easy—you need to take a bus to the Zhangzhou Port, take a twenty-minute boat ride to Xiamen, and then transfer by bus. The commute would take me more than two hours back and forth, and once, I had to stay in a shabby apartment because I could not afford to live in a hotel. Since I signed up for the TOEFL in July, I spent the entire month studying and preparing in the library. I would get up very early, go to the library, and stay there until the library was closed at night. Those days were certainly very tough, but I never complained because I knew this was what I had to do to achieve my dream to study abroad. Thankfully, my efforts paid off. I got 102 out of 120 in my first attempt, and the score was enough to apply for American universities.

Another thing that had a huge impact on my university life was the English speech contest. When I was a sophomore, I took part in the English speech contest at school. It was my very first time participating in such competition, and interestingly, in the first round, I gave my speech wearing sleepers. I can still remember the look on the judges' face when they saw my sleepers while I was walking onto the stage. One judge looked very indifferent to me the whole time. So after I gave my speech, I left because I knew that I would not make it to the next round. However, while I was walking on the stairs, I got a call from someone who told me that I had just made it to the next round of the competition. Although I only won the second prize in the final round, somehow the English teachers saw the potential in me, and they asked me to take some speech training.

At first, I did horrible in the training because, despite the fact that I had good pronunciation, I could not handle the impromptu questions—they were really difficult for me. But after some training and practice, I gradually got the hang of it.

In my second and third year, I took part in the English speech contests in the provincial level and won the second prize. Although I did not make it to the national level, I did not give up because I felt that I had a passion for it. I enjoyed speaking English in front of people, and winning the prize made me feel proud of myself. It gave me a sense of achievement that I did not have from studying. Eventually, in my final year, I made it to the national level (FLTRP Cup and *China Daily* cup) and went to Xiamen and the host city, Beijing, to take part in the competition.

The experience of taking part in the speech contests had really changed my life—it not only enriched my academic experience but also helped me improve my English significantly. But I think most importantly, it made me become more confident about myself.

You know, when you have achieved something (especially with the help of others), you tend to feel that it is important do something in return. That is the reason why I decided to start an English training club in my senior year. What I did was gather several members of the English department who spoke good English, and we were the first core members of the club. Then we tried to recruit new members in the department who desired to improve their spoken English. We came up with the name Ensanity because, at the time, Jeremy Lin, a former Asian NBA player, was quite famous, and we thought it would be interesting to combine the word *English* with *Linsanity*. So that was how we had this club name. The club met once a week, usually on Sunday night, to discuss current events and practice English speaking together. We also invited foreign teachers to come provide additional support. By the time I graduated from the university, we had over fifteen members, and this club went on even after I graduated.

In August 2013, my dream of studying in the USA finally came true. I was very lucky. Upon my arrival, Steve came to the airport to pick me up. We spent a few days together, during which he took me to supermarkets, restaurants, and his friend's farm, and he showed me some basic tips on living in a different country. After that, I flew to San Francisco.

In the orientation day, I met two Chinese students, Lai and Hui, and we became friends. One interesting thing was that Lai told us he was tutoring an American Chinese student who turned out to be my classmate. On that day, we were invited by a Chinese professor to a Christian gathering, and we met many Chinese students who also came to study in San Francisco State University (SFSU). We had dinner and played games together. I had a lot of fun, and I felt warm even in a foreign country.

I think making friends is quite important when you study in a foreign country. Like I said, I made friends with some Chinese students. We often hung out after class—dining out, watching movie, touring around the city, and so on. So I did not feel lonely or too nostalgic. I also joined the Chinese student association of the school and participated in many activities.

As a student, I deeply felt that the education in the United States was quite different from that of China. As a graduate student, I had only a few classes every week (I chose three to four courses each semester, and each course only met for three hours per week), which meant I had a lot of free time. But here in the United States, studying (or, rather, being an excellent student) requires a lot of discipline, meaning that you need to spend a lot of time doing homework, reading, researching, preparing for presentations, and writing essays.

In the first few months, I struggled to catch up with the lessons. Even though I did okay in the TOEFL, I had a hard time understanding the professors and my classmates when they were talking. I think it has little to do with the accent. Rather, I suppose it was because the way they talked was different from what you hear in the exams or recordings from textbooks. So it took me a while to get used to the style of lectures. Also, even though we did not have many classes, there was certainly a decent amount of homework to do. So I spent a lot of time in the library doing homework, and I even previewed textbooks, just to get myself ready for the next lesson.

Another aspect of American education was that classes were generally very dynamic and interactive. What I mean by that is, in China, many teachers teach in a sort of lecture style. They will use slides and PowerPoint while students listen and take notes. There is very little interaction between the teacher and the students. Students are reluctant to ask questions, even if they have one, just because they feel it is somehow disrespectful to the teacher, and it may interrupt the teacher talking. So students learn in a passive way. However, in the United States, teachers often ask questions to make students think. And students like to discuss and share their ideas. It is also quite common for students to interrupt the teacher and ask questions. Teachers actually welcome questions, and they are always happy to answer them. Besides group discussions, students will also do debate and presentations or even play games in class. Thus, I felt that the classes in the USA were much more interesting.

In addition to working hard on my studies, I also participated in some extracurricular activities. In my first semester, I volunteered in an ESL class where I coached some students (mostly Mexican immigrants) with their English. It was my very first time witnessing an authentic ESL class. I realized how learning a new language can be challenging for adults, especially for those who had learning difficulties. In my second year, I also tutored students and helped them with their English in an English learning center on campus, and I interned at American Language Institute and became an ESL teacher in my final semester. I continued teaching for one year before I returned to China.

If you ask me how it feels to be a teacher in the USA, I would say that it was certainly quite an experience. To begin with, the school did not just throw you a bunch of textbooks and materials and ask you to get ready for teaching. They asked you your preferences on subjects and how many courses you would like to teach, and they tried to make the best arrangement that suited every teacher's needs. Before you taught a class, you first tutored it. This meant that you had a chance to observe an experienced teacher teaching what you were going to teach next semester. There would be trainings throughout the semester—presemester training, weekly meeting, class observation, and so on. In a word, you would receive help on different aspects.

For example, in the presemester training, senior teachers shared their techniques in lesson planning, classroom management, and so on. Throughout the semester, you will meet with your course coordinator to discuss the curriculum, textbook content, and students. This was where they helped you understand the content in the textbook and gave you advice on how to execute teaching. When you had trouble students, they also told you how to deal with them. For the class observation, a senior teacher came into your classroom, observed, made notes, and recorded the lesson. You met afterward to discuss the lesson.

In addition to the help you received from senior staff, teachers often discussed with their colleagues the lessons and students, and they shared ideas and teaching techniques with one another. For me, the teacher office was not just a place to prepare for teaching but also a place to hang out with coworkers, chitchat, and relax. Another thing that is worth mentioning is that even though the place where I worked was a language training school, somewhat similar to the language institute here in China, we had a fixed teaching schedule every week, which meant that you would not need to teach a lot of classes, and you would not need to work extra hours.

About a month before returning home to China, I contacted one of my schoolmates in college and asked her about the job market in Xiamen. The reason was that she had been working in Xiamen since graduation, so she must know the job market very well. Also, I thought that Xiamen would be an ideal place to work because it isn't far from my hometown, Zhangzhou, and there were a lot of job opportunities. She told me she was teaching in a local language institute called Shinyway, along with another schoolmate. Interestingly, she also told me that I knew the principal, Oliver Wang, who was once my tutor back when I was teaching part time at New Oriental in the summer of 2014. What a coincidence. Immediately, we got connected, and he offered me a teaching position. So right after I returned to China, I went there for an interview and got the job. That was how I started my teaching career in China. Since then, I taught IELTS and TOEFL at Shinyway for four years.

Being a teacher at the institute was certainly demanding for me. To begin with, you got a lot of teaching hours. On average, I taught over 120 hours every month, and I worked six days a week. Mostly, I taught in the evenings and on weekends because that was when students left school and came for extra training on IELTS or TOEFL. But I think the worst part was that you did not get the whole vacation on holidays and festivals. The class size here was pretty small—usually less than six students. Besides, there was a lot of lesson preparation and homework grading. So I felt that work was my life at the time. But I did enjoy it. Preparing and teaching a new subject was exciting to me as it felt like exploring a new territory, and I was always fascinated by all kinds of textbooks—the context layout, pictures, exercises, everything. I also felt satisfied when my students got the exam grades they needed. My colleagues were really nice and friendly, and we became friends.

I decided to change my career path last year (2020) when my girlfriend got really sick. I realized that, all this time, I had been working, working, working and spent little time with her and my mother. (As I mentioned, I was busy teaching on festivals and holidays; so even though Xiamen was very close to my hometown, I only went home once or twice a year and spent no more than ten days in total.) I quitted my job and became an English teacher at a local international high school called Qunxian A-Level Program. In this school, students (mostly junior high graduates) spend four years studying International General Certificate of Secondary Education (IGCSE) and A-level courses and applied to study for a bachelor's degree in countries in the British Commonwealth of Nations.

Although I still teach English, I feel that it is quite different. Back at the Shinyway Language Institute, you taught by phase (around ten classes per phase); and after that, your students moved to the next phase, and you taught other students. But here, you teach by year, which is much longer. Sometimes you might even teach the same students from their first year till they graduate.

Also, I feel that the fundamental difference is that, in the institute, your primary responsibility was to help students improve their exam grades as soon as possible; but here in the high school, besides imparting knowledge, you should also help to build their character and shape their values. Many students come in with lazy attitudes and poor study habits. They might be late for class, disrupting the class by talking to their classmates or feeling sleepy in class, and they might not want to study at all. Thus, as a teacher, it is very important to make sure everyone is on task and that students are learning. Honestly, it isn't easy for me since I got used to just teaching the class and not having to worry about discipline issues; and in my first semester, I got frustrated very often when students disrupted the class. Also, as the headmaster of the class, I have to deal with a lot of trouble students like those fighting and returning to dorms late, and I need to communicate with their parents. So the transition is certainly quite challenging for me. But I believe that I will get used to it.

Some of you may have noticed that I did not pursue a teaching position in college. Well, the main reason was that, by the time I graduated from SFSU, the threshold of getting a teaching position in college is holding a PhD, but I have little interest in pursuing one. So I decided to start teaching and making money. Even though I did not achieve my dream of teaching in a university, for me, it does not matter because I am still teaching but in a different context.

Finally, I would like to express my sincere gratitude to Steve, who has been my mentor since college. It was him who gave me the inspiration and guidance. Without him, I would never have been able to study abroad and be teaching English today.

PART NINE:
TOGETHER
By MuYuan

My mother gave birth to me when she was thirty years old. She died when I was thirty years old. The day before she died, I had a dream about her. In the dream, she looked so healthy as if she had never been sick. Her hair was dark and smooth. Her face was radiant, and her cheeks were rosy. She stood there, looking at me with a smile. I would never forget how bright her eyes were. And no wheelchair was needed.

I woke up in my mother's hospital room with my heart racing. I had just been dozing off. My mother was in her bed next to my chair. She had a feeding tube going through her nose into her stomach, and an oxygen mask was over her mouth and nose. There was a urine catheter draining urine to a plastic bag hanging beside her bed. She also had wires attached to her chest, leading to a heart monitor as well as an oxygen monitor probe over her finger. She had no hair. It had completely fallen out after her last radiation treatment. Her face looked yellow and dry. Her feet were swollen. There was no color in her lips. She was in a coma.

I knew I just had a dream about her. My mother was saying goodbye in the dream and letting go. Because of this dream, I also knew that she probably was going to die in the next few hours or so. In fact, her body might still be alive, but her spirit had already gone. Mysteriously, I did not feel the sadness of separation in this dream but rather the joy of healing. I knew that our mother-daughter relationship might have come to an end in this life, but now we were closer than we had ever been before.

My mother and I both agreed that she was not a typical mother. Six years after getting married, she wanted no children. Remember, this was China in the 1980s. During this time, the one-child policy was just being implemented nationwide. Most families were adjusting to this new policy. It was probably much easier to find a woman who wished for more than one child rather than a woman who did not want children at all.

My mother did not realize that she had a pregnancy until she was three months pregnant with me. When she got her ultrasound report, she burst into tears. These were tears of distress. She did not want to become a mother. Of course, the rest of my family was very happy that a new life was coming.

Being pregnant with me was probably the second time when my mother felt like her life was out of her control since she had known my father. The first time happened when they were still dating. During that time, my father's younger sister committed suicide. This unexpected tragedy created a difficult situation for my father and mother. According to the cultural tradition in my hometown, when a death occurred in a family, direct family members who have plans to get married should either get married within one hundred days after the death happened or not marry anyone for the next three years. Because of this tradition, my father and mother's families decided that the young couple should get married immediately. My mother was reluctant. She did not want to get married that early, but she could not say no as it was also a time when dating was viewed the same as getting engaged. She did not have a reason to say no. Likewise, she did not have an option to say no to me, an unexpected life in her body.

During her whole pregnancy, she tried her best to hide her baby bump. When I was older, she repeatedly told me how much she did not like her baby bump and how much she could not understand why some pregnant women liked to show off their growing baby bump. She also hated hearing children cry. There is a baby story about me that I heard from her where I was left alone on a couch crying for three hours because she could not tolerate my cries.

When I was a child, I was mostly taken care of by my paternal grandparents. From Mondays to Fridays, I stayed with them at their apartment, and they would walk me to and from school. On Friday nights, my father would come pick me up so I could spend the weekends with him and my mother. Most of the time, I was resistant to leave my grandparents. I would grab a table leg, screaming, "I am not going!" Despite my resistance, I was taken away. Then on Monday mornings, my mother would take me to the kindergarten before she went to work. (My grandmother would come pick me up directly from her apartment at the end of day.)

But almost every morning, the Friday drama would replay, only this time with my mother. In front of my kindergarten, I would grab the nearest trash bin around me and cry, "Mama! I don't want to be here! I want to stay with you!" My cries were so loud that it successfully made me the center of attention in the midst of other toddlers and their parents or grandparents. This drama would not come to an end until my head teacher showed up and dragged me to the classroom.

For a very long time after entering my adolescence, I thought my mother and I were more like girlfriends rather than mother and daughter. We went shopping together. We shared clothes. She helped me do my homework so that I could go to bed earlier. Like most other adolescent girls, I was curious about sex and would ask her questions about it. She was open to my questions and encouraged me to ask her anything about my body. Being an only child in my family, I felt fortunate to have an elder sister relationship with my mother.

Things started to change when I moved to the States for graduate school. She became anxious that I had not been in a "real romantic relationship." I was disappointed that she was becoming a typical mother, like mothers of my other Chinese friends who kept asking, "When are you getting married?" In one of our quarrels about it, I told her that I did not see any reason to get married since she was not happy in her marriage herself. She responded to me, "That's it?

Then you are wrong. You will be leading a pathetic life if it's how you understand my marriage. Let me tell you. All marriages are the same. All couples eventually live with each other as if they were just roommates. Your father and I are not an exception."

The other time, she said, "I wish I had never sent you abroad. The emotional gap between you and me is getting wider. You are more westernized now. You only do things that make you happy. You don't think about doing anything to honor your parents."

During this time, I was still in a spiritual care training program in a hospital in Boston and had decided to apply to social work schools after my training. This decision brought big disputes between my parents and me. They had been uneasy that I was being trained in a hospital, doing what they considered as "death work," something that they felt like they could not brag about when their friends asked about me. They wanted me to apply to an administrative job at a Chinese airline, which was recruiting in Boston at that time. They believed that my high proficiency in English made me a perfect candidate for that job.

My fights with my mother over my future career path did not come to an end until I was accepted into a social work school. I also received a good scholarship package. I knew I would get it, but my parents never believed that a foreign student like me would get any scholarship in a field dominated by those from the States.

As I went through my first semester at social work school, my mother began to experience hallucinations and delusions. Finally, she was sent to the hospital and soon was diagnosed with meningioma, a type of brain tumor that is not considered cancerous. Still, the tumor was so large that it occupied one-quarter of her brain. The doctor warned that she might not survive the surgery.

I was working on my final papers at school when my father called me about my mother. He wanted me to fly home—as soon as possible. I calmly told him, "Everything will be OK. She will be fine." We ended the phone call. Then I collapsed in the hallway.

I flew home the same week. It was the first time I went home in three and a half years after coming to the States. Fortunately, my mother's surgery was successful. I stayed with her until she recovered from the surgery and then returned to the States to continue my studies. When I waved goodbye to her at the airport, she was full of tears as she always was; either it was me leaving home for college in the same city or she was going for a vacation abroad. None of us knew that over the next two and a half years, her brain tumor would transform into a cancer that would keep recurring. She would experience five more brain surgeries and six different types of radiation treatments. She would eventually die of the brain tumor and another cancer that had metastasized.

I came back home again after getting my master's degree in clinical social work. Initially, I thought I would only stay at home for several weeks. My mother got sick again shortly after I returned home. In the next one and a half years, my father and I spent most of our time either at home or in the hospital taking care of her. She became weaker and weaker. I did as many caregiving tasks as I could. I cooked for her. I fed her. I helped her take a shower. I accompanied her to the bathroom—when she was able to walk to the bathroom. I also fulfilled her old family roles, taking care of the family finances and keeping in touch with her friends. When I was doing these things, I had a strange feeling that somehow, in some ways, I had become my mother's mother. Surprisingly, I enjoyed how I felt about it.

I recalled her complaints about the emotional gap between us. She used to complain about me being cold to her, not showing my feelings toward her. At the same time, I was feeling desperate that no matter what I did to show her that I deeply cared about her (sending her cards, buying her gifts, texting her "I love you" endlessly), she would not acknowledge it. I felt like my new caregiver role was an answer to her complaints and her misunderstanding toward me as a daughter.

Two months before she died, a significant event happened between us. It was a sunny afternoon. My father was not at home. I lay next to my mother as she was napping. I was exhausted because of all the daily caretaking that my mother needed. I began to fall into sleep. Being half awake and half asleep, I heard my mother sing. Then I was being gently held by her. She let me rest in her arms. She kissed my forehead and whispered, "I love you so much, my baby." Tears began to fall in my heart. I knew that, as mother and daughter, we were both redeemed.

I stayed with my mother's body alone for a long time after she took her last breath. I carefully applied moisturizer to her face. When she was alive, she always liked it when I did that for her. She never said why, but I knew that she enjoyed the closeness between us when I applied the cream to her face. Then I walked her to the morgue in the hospital. I stayed with her in the funeral home on "spirit guarding night," which is the night before the funeral when family members hold vigil. It is said that the spirit of the dead person would come back home at this time. The next day, I spoke at her funeral service. I waited outside the crematorium when she was being cremated. When I saw her again, I only saw a skeleton of medium height. My brain went blank. It was a shocking experience that I have not yet comprehended.

A month after she died, I was looking through pictures on her phone. I found a picture of three pairs of slippers. These were slippers that she bought for my father, me, and herself. She put the slippers together and took a picture of them. I remembered how happy she was when she showed us the slippers because she thought they looked lovely. I suddenly realized, by looking at this picture, something about her that I was unable to understand before. I realized that what she had been seeking throughout her life was being together with family. Just like these three pairs of slippers being put together, it was important for her to see, to smell, and to feel the people whom she cared about. Coming from a broken family where she was sent away by her own mother to a strange city at a very young age, it was difficult—almost impossible—for her to maintain an emotional connection with people when there was a significant physical distance. She supported me to go abroad because, as a mother, she wanted me to grow. At the same time, she could not tolerate the long distance between us and was doing or saying things that, at the time, I thought were hurtful or confusing but really were out of her fear of "losing" me. What she wanted, in fact, was simple. She just wanted to be together with me, her daughter, whom she loved more than anything in this world.

I concluded my speech at my mother's funeral by saying, "Dear Mama, I know that you are still with me, only in a different form. I hope that, in your new life, you can do all the things you enjoy doing—traveling, painting, reading, etc. I will move on with your love and the memories about us. I will explore and experience this world for you. Please come see me. We will always be *together*."

PART TEN:
MY LIFE, A DREAM COME TRUE
By Jady Xianfeng Zhou

Chapter One

I always wonder what I really want. Till now, I am still wondering. I admit that I am a dreamer.

When I went to school for the first time, I was so happy and excited. It was my first time to make new friends and to know some new Chinese characters—so many first times. I never felt tired when I was a child in the daytime. I played games with my new friends—hide-and-seek, running, guessing game, and so on. Time went like a flash and never turned back. I miss those years so much. Looking back, it was just like a colorful picture embedded in my mind, so far away and so touchable.

Time and time again, I asked my mother where I am from. "You came from my belly, you lived in my body for nine months, and then I gave birth to you," she said. Confused by mother's answer, I gave up asking for a while; nevertheless, it never faded away.

I have a brother and a sister; I am the youngest in the family. Dad and Mom are peasants to the core. My mom worked industriously in the farm day after day, year by year. My father, in my memory, was a gambler and a lazy man. The struggle between my parents was a nightmare for me. I supported my mom from my heart, but I was so scared when my father got drunk; he might beat my mom, but I had no way to stop him. I just cried in the corner.

Life was just like a mess at that time. Every day when I returned home from school, I would do some homework. Sometimes I saw that my mom's eyes were red. I deeply knew the sorrow in her heart. She always tried to avoid eye contact with me. I was too young to comfort her, but I wanted to. The only thing I should do was study hard and get a high score in the final examination. I did.

My father had five brothers but no sister. My grandma thought it wasn't a perfect family. She desperately wanted a daughter. Grandma had a brother, but I never had the chance to know the man. He died at the age of forty-nine. He suffered four surgeries in his belly in three years. My poor grandma cried when she talked about the bitter past. I just listened quietly.

In May 14, 1985, I came to the world at a normal day. It was my mom's third child, and she told me I was born at noon. She also said it was the most painful birth she had ever suffered. Almost four kilograms, I was such a big boy; she was so happy.

My grandma told me an interesting story about my brother. It was on my birthday. He cried when he heard my mother screaming; he didn't know what was happening. He was extremely scared by the painful cry. He was only five years old.

I didn't know whether I would be a burden to the poor family. I don't remember how my parents raised me under that circumstance in the 1980s. The Chinese government put forward a birth control policy or the one-child policy, which meant my family would be fined for my birth. That was really a burden to my family. My parents had no money to pay the fine, and the government officials took a pig away from our house. That pig was the main income of my family. I really was a burden at that time—at least I thought so.

One month later, my aunt (wife of my third uncle; my father is the second) gave birth to a boy, and he was so lucky to be the first child of the family. I envied him so much. Anyhow, I got company to go to school every day. We studied in the same class, we were like brothers, and we hung out and played together. Unfortunately, he failed to go up to the next grade in the third year, and he felt so frustrated. The only thing I could do was to comfort him and give him a hug.

In 1990, my first uncle died of tuberculosis, and the whole family was in deep sorrow. I was too young to remember that day, and my grandma told me the whole story when I grew up. It is easy to heal the disease today, but it was fatal to human beings in the old days. I felt bad when I heard that, so I was determined to study science when I went to university. His wife refused to accept the truth, but she had to; she became a widow with three children. Life was tougher for her without my old uncle. People are so vulnerable, especially when we are faced with a terrible disease.

About one year later, my grandma asked my aunt whether she wanted to marry some man who might share the burden with her. She didn't want to. I can understand. To me, she was a great mother, and now she is a grandma herself. I don't know how she did it. Time flies.

In the spring of 1994, after the Chinese New Year, my parents decided to find a job in another province, which was a turning point for the family. That year, my brother and sister dropped out of school at the age of fourteen and thirteen, respectively. I had to stay at home. They discussed which family I would be staying with. I felt bad. Lots of thought crossed my mind. It was a complex situation. At last, I was informed that I would live together with my third uncle's family. My parents left home a few days later. They took my sister away. I didn't see them off and just locked myself in the bedroom; I cried for a whole day. My grandma persuaded me to join them for dinner. I felt hungry but ate nothing. I fell asleep early in the night. I found my pillow was wet when I woke up the next day. I remembered it was a cold rainy day. I missed my parents so much.

In the afternoon, I received the news that they arrived at the destination. I was happy. It was only a day since they left, but I felt they had been gone for a long time.

I had been counting the days since their leaving, increasingly getting used to living, eating, and sleeping without my parents. I focused on my studies. I was in my fourth grade, and I was doing well. My teachers liked me. At that time, a male teacher could beat a student who broke the school rule. There was an old teacher who was bald, tall, and very thin, and he was mean to students. We didn't like to see his ugly face. My Chinese teacher was a middle-aged woman whose daughter was in the same class as me. This girl was so beautiful, and I have to confess that I kind of liked her. We studied in the same class for the next four years until we graduated from middle school. We went to different high schools. I heard she had become a nurse four years ago. I regretted that I never said I liked her. I really did.

It was the winter of 1994, and the Chinese New Year was near, which meant I could see my parents, brother, and sister. It was very cold in the middle of China with no central heating. We just closed the door and burned charcoal to get warm. In the morning, I saw that all the roofs were covered with snow when I opened my sleepy eyes. Wearing clothes immediately, I ran out of the room to call on my neighbors from door to door. It was a fantastic day for us. We played snowball and chased one another. I liked to see the footprints behind me, which I called magic.

It was about to be winter holiday; we took the final examination (Chinese and math). I got high scores again, and I felt proud to show them to my parents. I thought that, in my heart, I started to count down the days by making some marks on the wall next to my bed when I would be seeing my parents again.

The day before my parents' return, I went to visit my maternal grandmother and got sick that day, so I had to stay the night there, expecting the next day to come quickly. I fell asleep slowly; it was an extremely cold night, but a warm, good dream took me through the darkness and away from illness.

The next morning, my brother came early with his old bicycle (a very important thing from my parents' marriage); it was older than me. I felt better when I got up, and then after a simple breakfast, my brother and I were on the way home on the bicycle. It was a snowy day, very cold, but it felt good to be close to my brother. I leaned on his back while my brother paddled fast. He knew how eager I wanted to be home and hold my dear mom. We had not seen each other for a whole year. Carrying me on the bicycle, I could see my brother's hair covered with snow. I was just watching his shoulder from the back, and he said nothing on the way. We said almost nothing to each other. No talking, just thinking silently.

After thirty minutes, we arrived. My family was waiting for us. I saw my mom in front of them. I couldn't stop my tears. I ran off the bicycle and held her tightly; we cried together. You can't image how happy I was at that time; my dad and sister came close to me and embraced me. My sister changed a lot in my eyes. I thought she was modern with her beautiful clothes; I kind of expected what they brought for me. I had a lot to tell them, but I didn't know how to express my feelings. My mother showed me a sweater; she made it herself. I couldn't wait to try it on.

It was the greatest New Year we had ever spent together. I got a red envelope (*hong bao*) on New Year's Eve of 1995. It was big money for me. The fireworks were so wonderful that night as I was looking to the sky and having a deep breath. What a way to be with my parents, brother, and sister to begin a new year.

Chapter Two

The Chinese New Year is the best time to satisfy your stomach in the countryside, especially for us kids. Every family, rich or not so rich, spent lots of money to treat their relatives with good dishes because it was a special time to dine together; if you treated us today, it would be our turn next time. This is Chinese hospitality.

Every family owned a round table (it means togetherness and unity with relatives or friends) that meant best wishes to all of them who ate food around it; ten people shared one table. Usually, there were two special seats for VIPs; that was a tradition, and people never broke it. Sometimes the dishes were ready, but there were just seven or eight people who just kept their eyes on the delicious food; if anyone started with the chopsticks, the VIP would stare at him/her with a special meaning for a long time. Nevertheless, I enjoyed the holiday every year.

The happiest time passed by so fast; to spend more time with the family, I hardly left home to play. I knew in my heart my parents and brother and sister would depart again, with me staying behind without them. My mother seemed to read my mind; sometimes I pretended to be happy, even though I felt really sad deep inside. I knew I must accept the reality.

My parents made some money by working hard in their first year; that was good news and meant we would have a better life if they went out working again. For me, it was a dilemma; and at last, they made the decision for me to live with my third uncle's family for another year.

The day when they left, I didn't lock myself in the room and came to see them off. I understood it was hard for them too. It was late afternoon, the bus was coming, and the departure time was getting closer and closer. I couldn't help but weep but tried to stop the tears. They got in the bus with a smile; they tried not to cry. The bus left before sunset; it faded away, and I prayed for them.

I had to wait another year to see them. It was hard for me, a ten-year-old boy. It was my last year to study before going to middle school, which meant I could enjoy the last International Children's Day in my life. That day was hot; with the beautiful white T-shirt, I stood in the crowd, and we got candies and cookies from school as we did in the past four years. The difference was it would end after today. I sweat a lot because we stood in a line for a long time to get the special presents. I didn't complain; I loved the day.

I never imagined I could live in this beautiful campus beside the seashore. I heard about sea from the book I read and saw from the TV. Today I could see the seashore anytime I wanted to; it was like a dream had come true. "No pain, no gain." I like that motto. Who created the opportunity for me to realize it? It was just a question.

I graduated this year, and after the summer holiday, I went to middle school with many students I had never met before, and so making friends was the first entrance course we should take. There were many kinds of courses including chemistry and physics, especially English, which made me think of white people with big noses and black people with white teeth. My English teacher was a charming young lady; she had an elegant voice. I was pleased to be one of her students. At first, I was interested in this exotic course—A, B, C . . . X, Y, Z. All of us spent three weeks pronouncing and reciting them (the twenty-six letters); it was difficult for me. I had never experienced that. I didn't know what the hell they really meant. I confess that I kind of wanted to retreat; however, I didn't.

There was an examination when we finished studying from A to Z. I got an A+; the teacher gave a red star to praise those who got an A or A+, and I was encouraged to study harder. We began to study some simple dialogues in the class, like saying "hello" in English. We often used the Chinese way of pronouncing English words, and that meant I could not speak fluently in English because of bad pronunciation. There were no native speakers in my small town till today. So we hardly had a chance to compete with the children living in the city. I envied their better situation than that of our poor children. I felt there was no fairness in the world. I always believe that, but I know you must study harder and harder to change your future. You cannot change your fate by doing nothing. Just have faith and keep being confident and optimistic.

The school changed our English teacher for some reason, and we got a new one who was a fat middle-aged guy looking very serious about anything. Evidently, we didn't like him very much. After his first course, we found his son in our class. This guy bullied the girls. He was taller than most boys in this class. His father never did anything about his son. I started to hate the teacher and his fucking son. My English score plunged a lot in the semester.

I was hoping to move to another class, but it never did happen. I had no choice but to accept the reality. Many classmates didn't like that fat guy either.

So most of them had experienced something I experienced. I felt good not having to face him and his son alone. We started to sleep in the English classes or even skipped them. We did that knowing we could be punished. The semester was about to be over, and I was facing a tough time. I might fail to get through to the next grade, and that would be a shame. I failed the English exam, but I was safe and went to the next grade. "Whoa!" I screamed in excitement. The most important thing was the fat guy would be gone in my life, and I would get a new English teacher. It didn't matter who that new teacher would be. It could not be worse than the fat guy.

It was too difficult for me to catch up with others after stopping practicing English for a whole term. I had to study harder than others till my graduation. My parents hoped for me to go to a good high school. I didn't want to disappoint them.

But as I had said, it was too hard. I was trying. In the end, I failed to go to a good high school in the city but a normal one in my county. I knew I disappointed both my father and mother when I gave the call to tell them about that. They didn't blame me but gave me courage to fight for a better life (leave the poor land and fly as high as I can). I cried when I hung up the phone. That was the fourth year my parents worked in another city.

It was my first time to leave my hometown for the county. I had never been to the county since the day I went to high school. I was just like a frog in a well, satisfied with a small space. However, I had changed a lot since the day I saw the difference between the countryside and the city. I eventually understood what my parents told me. Many things were new to me in the city—bus, supermarket, red and green lights at every intersection.

The whole three years of studying was for the college entrance examination (CEE) in China. Students must study six days per week, regardless of whether it was summer or winter, almost one thousand days in this "war." I was short and thin when I studied for the first semester, and then I began to play basketball with my friends. I was always a substitute because I was short and thin, and that made me mad at them inside. I kind of grew up since the summer holiday, and I marked on the wall to record my height every week. That was crazy. But I hoped not to be a substitute anymore.

After the holiday, that would be my second year to study, and it was getting closer to the CEE. During the second year, something happened to me; a girl fell in love with me, and I didn't know it at first. But I experienced something that was new to me. I was so dull to feel love at that time, and the girl would send and leave a message in my book. She did this to me every day. I felt something wrong, and finally, she told me the truth face-to-face one night. I declined to accept her to be my girlfriend. I said something like I had to study hard, and I didn't want to be distracted by anything else. She turned back and left. The next day, I heard she cried for a long time with another girl who lived in the same dorm with her. I was upset and afraid to see her again. What would happen if we met each other again? Many thoughts crossed my mind. Eventually, she applied to another school in the same county not far away; but since that day, we never met again till I graduated.

In 2003, I took the CEE. Days and years went by silently; three years were just like a wink. The only thing you can do is to take the wheel and steer by yourself and move forward for a better life no matter how tough it will be.

In 1983, my grandma lost her husband, my grandpa.

Chapter Three

At eighteen years old, I was not a child any longer, and becoming an adult meant I would be responsible for the outcome of my behavior. This was a big time of my life. The eighteen years just flew by like a flash. What I owned and what kind of benefit I brought to my family confused me sometimes. After I graduated from high school, I had to find a way to pursue my dream that would lead me to a whole new level. But I knew in my heart nothing could stop me from flying high in the sky like an eagle.

In my hometown, there were a few people who had a so-called good education. Many young boys and girls dropped out of school because of poverty, or their parents wanted them to take over their job as farmers. That was sad and pathetic. Now there was a chance in front of me after high school; the strong desire to pursue a better life was just like a thirsty dog begging for some cold, clean water. I cannot believe I compared myself to a dog.

The summer was tough for me because every day I saw my parents working hard for subsistence and for me. My father stopped gambling and drinking and worked hard to make money to pay for my tuition. His back began to bend. My mother was a typical Chinese country woman, hardworking and simplehearted. That was my dear mom, who sacrificed her whole life for her children.

One time when I spotted a cluster of gray hair beside her ear, I felt bitterness in my soul. I was determined to create a better life for her with my hands. At that moment, I found that I grew up and became a man. I knew what my responsibility would be.

Life is not simple like we see in a naive way; it is more complicated than you can imagine, but I have faith that every cloud has a silver lining. It depends on the way you value the world and yourself; sometimes you need someone to guide you to the right direction when you are lost. You cannot choose your family, but at least you can pick your friends. Fate is in your hands; hold it firmly and sometimes give it some fresh air. The dream is in your heart; protect it with your hand and sometimes give it some space to fly.

The place I grew up in was a small town; hundreds of people had guarded the holy small land from generation to generation for hundreds of years, and nobody wanted or dared to leave for the fantastic world outside. Maybe it would be hell for them, who were used to living a poor, simple life. I recall the first time I went to the city where I went to college. The crossroads drove me crazy because crossing a road alone was hard for me. It was terrible. I totally had no idea about red or green light, just like a wild animal coming out from the mountain.

In September, I registered as a university student, and it was a bittersweet feeling when I handed in the money to the office. It was a big money that my parents had worked and saved for a whole year. I just couldn't get this thought out of my mind for the whole day. I doubted if it was worthwhile to spend this money. I was so innocent and naive.

After registration, I moved forward to the dorm area and found my room. It was dirty, and the smell made me vomit. I saw a big gray rat rushing by when I opened the door, and it scared me. What a surprise to me! I began cleaning the room and my bed after putting all my luggage down. I really felt it was not fair for me to clean the room alone because there were seven beds left.

The first night was scary and lonely because I was the only one in the room. I felt empty and hoped that somebody would come to this room to find a bed. Nevertheless, nobody showed up until the next morning. But at least I thought that it was an important experience to be independent, leaving parents and close friends. I gave a call to my parents to tell them I was all right the next afternoon. They were excited and asked me a lot of questions about eating and sleeping and told me to take care of myself. I knew I was a spring chicken in their mind, and I would always be. I understood their good wishes.

All the beds were occupied in three days; everybody introduced themselves to the others for a few minutes. A new home of brothers was founded that night, and it was amazing to see so many strange faces. And I didn't feel lonely anymore. The room was not dirty and empty any longer. I had a fantastic dream that night; I encountered a beautiful girl in some corner and fell in love with her. I couldn't help thinking about the blurry but good-looking face I had seen in my dream.

After the enrollment of freshmen, we participated in compulsory military training. I had heard about it; it aimed to train the students' body and spirit, but it sounded scary because we had to stand stiffly under the sun for several hours. Obviously, it was a torture for my vulnerable body because of lack of nutrition. What drove me crazy was that the training would last for half a month. How could I accept that reality? However, I had no choice but to adjust to the painful days.

Finally, I successfully survived the damning training and benefited from it. I learned a lot through teamwork and helping one another. Most importantly, the class to which I belonged won a prize based on our team efforts, and we did a good job. I was so proud and happy.

All those things happened like yesterday in my memory. I will never forget that wonderful moment in my life.

The campus life started with a military training in every college all over China. I liked this kind of beginning because it made me stronger both in body and mind. Through this, we could know one another better and deeper, and it was easier to build relationships.

I quickly concentrated on studying. I knew which way I should go. Working hard made me feel fulfilled and satisfactory every day and night. I liked falling asleep so fast after a whole day of studying. Sometimes I went to neverland far away, sometimes I dreamed of my diligent and hardworking parents bending their back working in the field, and sometimes I thought of my mother's best dishes. Unfortunately, I would have to wait for half a year to taste those dishes again. So I began to count down how many days were left to go home.

The first semester went by fast. I learned a lot about how to behave in public. I was not afraid to cross the street by myself. I knew the importance of being aggressive and ambitious. I realized for the first time where my destination was. "Grab every opportunity if you have a chance" became my motto in life. I knew I was not a boy anymore, so I shaved my virgin mustache to look like a man. The dream to become a grown-up in my childhood had come true.

Chapter Four

College life added a lot of spice into my veins. I absolutely adjusted to that environment and enjoyed it. My major was biotechnology, and we got so many basic theories to learn in the first two years. I admit that I really worked hard like in high school.

I clearly realized that life was not only about studying and staying in line; sometimes I needed some space to imagine and dream. I had to save a cell in my soul for them. I did not want to be a stiff guy who often was the target of teasing. Failing in the entrance examination was like a heavy stone that made my life so rough. I was a third-year student, but I didn't feel dispirited because I owned a lion heart. I was more independent than my peers as my parents left me to earn money for almost ten consecutive years.

My English sucked when I came into the campus. The first English class seemed so long and hard. My English teacher, an elegant middle-aged woman, randomly picked me twice to spell new words. My tongue tied like there was a butterfly in my mouth. I failed to make a good first impression on her. The low-level countryside education did not give me a chance to practice my English. Jesus Christ! It was the longest forty-five minutes that I ever experienced in the classes. How I can improve it became the theme of the week. I knew I could overcome all troubles to be better at it. Wait and see.

Let bygones be bygones; refreshing the soul and moving forward was the real mission. I must stand up when I was down like a real man. I was twenty-two, healthy, and passionate. Nevertheless, life brought some surprises to me rain or shine. Also, my life was not only taken up with studies, but how to spend the spare time was a real problem for me. I would take that into consideration. I just wanted to make my life interesting and meaningful, and I outlined some plans. Being a part-time tutor to make some money was the top priority; it was a win-win job. I got the money and social experience. I should focus on the students' progress and maybe high scores. Can you imagine? Being a tutor was the most attractive job for students. I knew it. I was there.

So naturally, it became more and more competitive. It was time for advertising and posting job notices everywhere. Some guys even built a team (four to five members) to improve the marketing. It was obviously a brain battle. What could I do in such a bad atmosphere? Extensive advertising was a must if you hoped to survive. There were so many ways to draw people's attention, especially parents of twelfth-grade students and rich families. The memory of that time never faded away.

One particular episode is worth telling. Du, one of my roommates, was also a job hunter. One day he got up very early, and with a pile of leaflets, he began to post his advertisement in every corner to get people's attention. But unfortunately, on his way back to the campus, he was intercepted by two city inspectors, and they took Du to the police station in the name of violating the public environment. Oh god, you can imagine how scared he was, and so he immediately confessed everything he had done. Finally, they released him out of the hearing room without penalty but on the condition that they confiscate his cell phone and the rest of the leaflets. He had to write a self-criticism letter with the college's stamp to redeem it.

We could not help but laugh after hearing his pathetic story; however, that lesson made us more careful when conducting this kind of mission. I had to penetrate into the communities at night, carefully and quietly gluing the leaflets on the wall of each apartment. Then I just waited for the phone to ring. That was it. All the leaflets were self-made during my spare time. What I wrote on the leaflet was simple: "My name is Zhou Xianfeng. I am a sophomore with major in biotechnology. I am good in English and math teaching." My idea was using the least cost to make the biggest profit. The business didn't last for a long time, but I did earn some money to pay for my everyday expenses.

There was a very important part that I almost forgot to tell, and it was about my love story. I have shared my love stories with several of my close friends, but some parts are buried in the bottom of my heart for many years. I fell in love with a lovely girl at first sight. It was a sunny afternoon, and I was walking out of the classroom after finishing all my homework. I encountered one of my female classmates, Huang, and beside her was a pretty girl. We said hello to each other and departed, but her face never left my mind. This feeling was hard to tell, and I was hit by it, so I was looking forward to seeing her again. The second day, something surprised me. Huang told me that the girl had the same feelings for me and asked for my name. What a day!

I got the phone number of Huang. I chose the perfect time to call her. We had a good time talking. It was a good beginning. She said she would come visit me the following week. And I couldn't wait to see her. Friday was coming, and I could hardly focus on my lessons. She finally called me and said she was already in the campus. I rushed to the gate to find her. I still remember her beautiful face and smile. Honestly, I kind of hoped to skip that part, but the picture in my mind didn't allow me to do this. So I want to just be natural and follow my heart in telling this story.

Love came so fast that I was not really prepared to accept it. But I had no reason to refuse that beautiful moment. One day, and just one day, we went into a relationship, and we were serious about this decision. It is always easy to make out some spark between fresh lovebirds; without exception, we fell into love with each other. Love was a really magical stuff to me. It gave me inspiration and passion to do the brave things that I never had a chance to do. Nevertheless, we just met each other once or twice per week because we were in different colleges. So I had to call her every night before going to bed. It cost me a lot to use the phone, so I had to save my money for this purpose. So pathetic. Looking back, I found we were not the perfect pair. There were so much conflicts and disagreements between us, and they could hardly be resolved by just a simple call.

This relationship died in a special way that I didn't want to tell. Even though it just lasted for two months, I still found many shining spots in this journey of first love. Learning how to let go is very important when it doesn't belong to you. There are many ways to success, and so do not put all the eggs into one basket, even if it is love.

Chapter Five

After our breakup, I soon recovered from it and concentrated on my studies. As a sophomore at the time, I told myself not to develop another relationship with any girl. The truth was I could not control myself and started another relationship. I utterly lost in this battle; regret was the only feeling I had in the next months.

This relationship began just because I was softhearted, and she was a girl I met in the campus cyber room. She was experiencing the worst time of her life, having an abortion and then breaking up with her ex. I confessed that I just showed her my compassion when I heard about it, but she needed more, which I gave to her in the end. This kind of beginning was doomed to have a tragic ending, and the facts proved this point of view.

First love was beautiful, but I won't compare these two relations with two different girls. What I learned was facing the music no matter what kind it was. There are so many passersby in my life journey, but just a few can really walk into my life to influence my blueprint. I feel thankful to them for teaching me how to make decisions and choices in the future. Bitter and sweet are both real elements of love and life, so I'd like to accept all the consequences that I cannot change. Life shouldn't stop merely because of a stumbling block, so let's learn the lesson, move on, and hope for the positive.

In the new semester of 2005, I was informed that I passed the CET6, a turning point for me to revalue my ability and plan for postgraduation. As one of the assistants, we had to help the freshmen finish their registration in the first day until they moved into a dormitory. I had a crush on a girl whom I rarely saw in the past two years because I spent too much time studying. During the registration, I had a chance to get close to her. I was encouraged to borrow her Walkman and then had a short conversation with her. I also felt she had some good feelings for me. After that, we spent more time talking about life and the future. I found we had many things in common about our values and our future.

We both majored in biology, and going for advanced education was a priority for most students like us. Then we got the consensus to take the postgraduate examination and prepared for it. I guessed that might be a sign she was willing to take me seriously, and I was right about it.

But our parents were 100 percent opposed to it; they said we shouldn't develop a relationship before graduation. In their minds, studying was the top priority for us in the campus instead of wasting time to chase after love. So we must pretend in front of them when we returned home during summer vacation or the Chinese spring festival. During this time, we kept contact by texting or calling when we were alone. The holiday was over, and we returned to college. I couldn't wait to see her and kiss her. We maintained the relationship till I graduated in July 2006, but she got the last year ahead. So we would take the postgraduate exam but not together and in different cities.

My fifth uncle helped me find a job in Zhejiang Province in the east of China. "You should have a job to support yourself. Meanwhile, try to make use of your spare time to prepare for the examination," he said to me. Of course, he did not know I had a girlfriend. I accepted his help after I obtained my girlfriend's support. I knew, in her heart, she hoped we would stay together to face that difficult time.

I left the campus for the job destination in August. I'll never forget the day I left. After packing all my stuff and having lunch together, we spent about an hour comforting and encouraging each other. It was time to catch the train, so we went out to get a taxi. Having a tough time looking into her eyes, I choked back my tears till I closed the car door. In the rearview mirror, I saw her crying in the fading shadow. It was the first time I strongly felt the pain of departure.

Chapter Six

Getting into the train that would head to a new destination for me, I felt a little upset about my future life. I guessed I was not completely ready for this sudden turning point, but I had to face it and overcome this kind of negative emotion. It was the first step that each graduate student would encounter and also a very important journey of our life cycle.

The train was supposed to arrive in Jianshan City at about eight in the evening, and there would be a company car waiting for me. The train finally stopped in the Jiangshan rail station at eight thirty. I went off the coach and moved to the exit gate. There was a white car, and I walked very fast toward it, even though I was so tired. They recognized me very soon, and then I shook hands with everybody including the middle-aged driver. The car took us to a restaurant, and we had a dinner together. I felt warmhearted by their welcome and entertainment, so I drank a lot of beer to show my gratitude.

The next morning, what was waiting for me was a brand-new environment and many strange people. The company supplied me a living room to go through the transition period, which meant a lot to me as a poor student. Without friends and relatives, I had to cope with everything all by myself. That was OK for me, an independent left-behind boy since I was nine or ten years old when my parents left home to earn money. I knew how to get along with people around me, even when they were new to me. I also knew how to analyze and resolve problems and distinguish good from bad.

Time flew by like a flash. I received my first salary; the transition was too fast for me to transfer my role between a student and a social worker. It was an exciting moment, and I shared it with my girlfriend thousands of miles away from me.

I made a strict time table to prepare for the examination when I settled down in this city, working from nine to five and then studying from six to eleven or twelve o'clock. With almost no weekend, now I am proud to say that I insisted on my plan for half a year till the examination day. The sacrifice was worth it to me, even though I failed to get through. "No pain, no gain." I like that motto.

Waiting for fate's decisive result was an unpleasant experience, and I had to wait for two months till the score was available on the internet. I would never forget the moment when I clicked the Enter key. "Yes! Yes, I made it! I did!" I cried alone for a while; it was like a dream come true. The score was 341; to tell you the truth, I like the number so much. I was going to Xiamen University for an interview. It was located near the Pacific seashore with a beautiful scenery and clean air. I longed for this city from the day I applied for the examination, and now I could not believe I got a chance to realize my dream.

I knew what this interview would mean to me in this special time of my life; a new chapter was ahead of me if I succeeded in getting through it. Without any experience, the only thing I could do was do the best in preparation. The interview was approaching, and I was ready for the journey. I left in advance for almost a week. I didn't go straight to Xiamen but to my campus, where my girlfriend was still studying. I hadn't seen her for several months till that time. The last time we met was the new year. It was she who came to visit me and spent two or three days with me. It was her longest travel since her birth. Seeing her after a long time was always exciting for me.

My parents were more excited and proud than anyone when they got the news. What they could do was support me from the bottom of their hearts. I needed their support. Nevertheless, I got to the last step to change my life, so it was the best time for a celebration.

There were many students on the campus who also passed the examination. So my next target was to communicate with them about the interview. Unfortunately, she failed to pass the exam, and so she put a high expectation on me. It was a battle I couldn't lose. I really treasured this opportunity.

My girlfriend helped me pack everything I needed for this interview, which started my journey to the beautiful seashore city. "Xiamen, I am coming."

Chapter Seven

Next morning, I arrived at the Xiamen railway station after a night sleeping in the train. Finally, I landed in the fantastic city to get my master's degree for the next three years. My major was microbiology, and that would determine my future or career to some degree.

Looking back, I found there were several important things I have to tell you. First was hard learning and study. My tutor was a fifty-plus-year-old man who handed over a lot of experiments to me for his megaproject, a novel natural product that can potentially confine a breast tumor. I learned a lot from the project. Second, in the second year, I began to join the English corner, where I met several exchange students from the USA and Ukraine. We hung out several times. Increasingly, my oral English improved. Plus, each day I would spend an hour watching the American sitcom *Friends*. I could now communicate using English. Brick by brick, my English soared like magic.

One other thing is my privilege of having met an American visiting professor. It changed or shaped some aspects of my life. I first met him in the campus bus stop. After stepping into the same bus, we began to talk. He showed some interest in me, and I left him my email in case we had no chance to see each other again.

There were several things about Steve. I carefully read his first book *For My Hands Only*. I was touched by the story of his life and learned who he is, where he is from, what he experienced in childhood and in high school, and then his chase after his dream in Singapore and the USA. He supported me a lot in many ways, and I owe him and thank him for helping me through some tough times. He has published eight books, and I am proud of him.

So life in Xiamen, in general, was simple and busy. After getting my degree, it was time to get a decent job. After receiving a number of offers, I chose Nanchang CDC for two reasons. My girlfriend had waited for me for three long years in the city, her hometown. We planned to get married. Also, I would be near my parents. That simple.

Life in Nanchang was tough for the first two years, and the salary was low, not enough to support the wedding. In these two years, I worked hard in my daily job and kept improving my English day after day. Anyway, we made the decision to get married after much thought. In the beginning of 2012, we got married. In June, a big news came from my wife—she got pregnant. Exciting, indescribable feeling filled my head. In March 2013, our son Eric added joy to our simple life. In the same year, I got promoted as deputy section chief; and later, I got a scholarship from Japan-China Medical Association to study in Tokyo as a visiting scholar. When I left for Japan, Eric was about one year old.

Tokyo life totally changed my many thoughts and my attitude toward Japan and its people. China and the Chinese could learn many things from Japan. After one year of visiting, I made a lot of progress in research, and then my tutor recommended me to do a PhD degree. I applied for a PhD fellowship from the Japanese Society for the Promotion of Science (JSPS). After two years of working hard, I was awarded a scholarship to pursue my PhD in Japan.

Our second child—a girl, Coco—was born while I was studying in Japan. She brought us joy and happiness as a family. Life goes on and on with so many challenges and tough moments. I have a family now, and we are all healthy. Our country is becoming stronger. Now we are able to support our parents and our own family. The kids are growing up happier than me, and they have more chances to make mistakes and try new things like music and sports.

Looking back the past thirty-six years of my life, I have plenty to thank for. But we have more to do and think to make this world a better place for our children. First, we need to conquer COVID-19 so our lives will improve.

PART ELEVEN:
I TALK TO MYSELF, STEVE
By Roy Qi Cai

Part 1: Desperation

In 2006, I was a sophomore in high school. And at the time, I was—like many of my teenage school friends—crazy about computer games. With our dear pocket money, we would play computer games at the nearest computer bar or café outside my campus. Yes, it was not a good thing to do because it affected my studies and caused poor academic performance. Shockingly, my rank dropped from the 40th to 380th. By the way, there were about 700 students in my grade.

One day after learning of my poor exam results, I walked out of the campus with a broken heart and went for lunch. Full of resentment and annoyance about myself, I walked into a restaurant and had my lunch silently. You would think all my hope and desire to enter a college was destroyed and ruined. I did it to myself.

Part 2: Inspiration

While pretending to enjoy my simple noodle lunch, out of nowhere, I suddenly heard some music from the TV, followed by an English monologue. Like some fresh air blowing through the restaurant, I suddenly woke up from my sadness and sorrow and began to listen carefully to every word in the monologue. Fifteen years later, I could still remember what happened at that restaurant and what happened to me. Believe it or not, I could still remember every word and recite the same monology today like some of my college friends could recite the famous "I Have a Dream" speech by the famous black American, Martin Luther King.

> Hi, I'm Gilbert Arenas and this is my story. When I first entered the NBA, the first forty games of my

career, I sat on the bench. They said I was gonna play zero minutes. You know, I just think they didn't see the talent that I had. They thought I was a zero. Instead of sitting there being bitter, I just practiced, practiced. If no one believes in you, anything you do is a positive. It wasn't even about basketball anymore. It was about proving them wrong. Now the reason I wear number zero is because it lets me know that I need to go out there and fight every day.

Like being hit by lightning, I trembled, raised my head, and looked at Arenas on the TV, feeling that he was speaking to me personally. And I heard every single word of his monologue. *How lucky I am*, I thought. He was talking to me at the right time and at the right place. I felt like someone somewhere knew what was happening to me in my life. Yes, you know I had heard too much disappointments from my parents. But this monologue was different. I felt encouraged and inspired and believed I could have another chance to do something with my life.

And the voice wasn't from someone I knew in my life. It was from a foreign stranger in a TV commercial that I had never seen before. Yes, now it reminded me of what my American professor often said to us in his classes in college. "Everything happens for a reason."

It is never too late, is it? Now it is about the courage to prove everyone is wrong about me. Yes, it is time to go out there and fight every day. Practice, practice, practice. Yes, Gilbert Arenas, when no one believes in you, anything you do is a positive.

Part 3: Passion

After that, I began to recite Arenas's words in my mind over and over again. When eating, walking, and before sleeping, it seemed these words were deeply imprinted in my mind, like inhaling fresh air in early spring, like drinking a cold drink in the middle of a hot summer.

But intuitively, I also started to develop a habit of *talking to myself.* Because the advertisements was in English, I used it religiously in my daily oral English practice, not once but hundred times each day, like a Buddhist monk chanting his prayers at a sacred altar in a mountain temple for students who desperately hoped to enter the best university in China or for the rich departed souls, like the Christians reading the chapters and verses of their Bible daily, or like the Muslims reciting their daily prayers facing Mecca.

It had helped me develop a good sense of English. My daily practice went beyond merely reciting Arenas's words. I would talk to myself, ask myself questions and answer myself, imagine myself in various situations, and push myself to try to say something in English. Of course, I also started to pay attention to the basketball player Gilbert Arenas and watching NBA games. And slowly, like an innocent teenager addicted to computer games, I actually became a huge fan of Washington Wizards. The pronunciation of the Chinese name for Wizards is exactly the same as my name's pronunciation (Qi Cai).

Yes, everything happens for a reason; but as an incurable Chinese brought up in my rich culture and tradition, I think this is what the Chinese have always said. "This is your destiny or fate." Yes, I deeply believe in it.

And after a semester of crazy practice, I could pronounce many English words accurately and fluently and read an English article of two or three thousand words without difficulty. Even though this article contains a lot of English words that I did not learn in class, my profound love of English and enthusiasm for Arenas drove me to learn more and more each day.

For a ninety-minute English test, I would often need thirty minutes to complete it, and the accuracy rate was above 90 percent. I began to realize that as long as I put in more effort than ordinary students, I could easily achieve my goal. And if this could happen to English subjects, then it must be the same for other subjects. Like a desperate person seeing the light of dawn, I ignited my spirit and was determined—rain or shine, hail or storm—to face my miserable academic performance and fight back.

I got up at five o'clock to do morning reading and would read and recite English texts passionately. I could also face the brain-racking math and study until eleven o'clock in the evening. This passion lasted almost the whole final year of my high school.

Part 4: Answer to the Question

The results also proved that my efforts were not in vain. My performance ranking jumped from 380 to around 80. In the end, my college entrance examination results allowed me to enter the TKK College of Xiamen University, a second-tier university in China. What a relief!

At TKK College, I met my mentor and friend Steve. After a short time, I took the initiative to find him and talk to him in English. After some conversations, he was surprised by my fluency in spoken English. I was the only student in class who impressed him the most with my spoken English simply because most students were unable to speak any English, though they majored in English.

"So what did you do to improve your English, Roy? You told me you came from a small town with no computer bar or café. Obviously, there was no one in your little town who could speak English to or with you. I am curious. How did you improve your spoken English? How on earth did you practice your spoken English?" I talked to myself thousands of times.

And Professor Steve would take every opportunity to share this with the students in his English classes, and he would demonstrate how it is done or what it means to talk to yourself. I was totally impressed. I just hope my experience will be an inspiration to all the students who aspire to be fluent English speakers, like native speakers of English.

"If no one believes in you, anything you do is a positive."

PART TWELVE:
I WANT TO STUDY ENGLISH IN
THE UNIVERSITY
By Ruby Wei You

I am You Wei in China or Wei You in the West. In my country, China, the family name is written first. My English name is Ruby. I was born in 2002 in Qianjiang, a rural town located in the southeast of Chongqing, Sichuan Province.

Both my mother and my father are migrant workers, and to make money, like many Chinese parents, they went to work in a big city, Guangdong, Guangzhou Province. And I became a left-behind child living with my grandpa. When I was about three years old, Grandpa took me to live with my parents in Guangdong. I considered myself very lucky to live with my parents. I saw an amusement park for the first time in my life. I saw many novel things that were absent in my hometown. My new experiences broadened my horizon.

Unfortunately, because of the *hukou* system in China, I had no choice but to return to live with my grandpa at the age of six. If I were to continue to live with my parents and because of my rural *hukou* in China, I would not be able to attend an urban school or apply for any social services meant for children who had urban *hukou*. My parents had no choice but to send me back to our hometown and live with Grandpa.

Even though my parents did not have a good education in their lives, they were very strict with my studies. In their view, working hard is the most important key to a promising future. They believe in education. And when I was in primary school, I was asked to recite one Chinese text or a poem every day, including the weekends. I would complain, but I really learned a lot. I was able to improve my memory and develop good study habits. It had influenced my whole study life as a student.

I started studying English when I was in junior high school. I assume primary school English is not popular nor required where I grew up. Truthfully, it was difficult for me to learn a new language. At first, I spent much time learning and speaking the phonetic or pinyin English. It took some time to shift to the real English with the English alphabet. Fortunately, I had very caring and patient English teachers, and they assisted me with my English learning.

I was lucky to have Mary Pu as my high school English teacher. And it was Mary Pu who taught us how to learn English properly. She trained us to divide complex sentences to understand the meaning. She also taught us to write an English essay or article by focusing on certain key words. I was lucky to have her in my high school, and I truly appreciated her care for our English learning and proficiency in high school.

I would say life in high school was the most meaningful to me. Everyone focused on preparing for the university entrance examination. You could say it was a period of sorrows and joys. Physics was a difficult subject for me. Sleep was the biggest problem. I had to face stress and low spirits. It was a mix of sorrow and happiness. And when I was about to give up, family, friends, classmates, and teachers were always there to save me from drowning. I consider myself a sensitive person, and without all of them, I could not have achieved the score I wanted and required to enter the university.

For most Chinese parents, the college entrance examination would determine a child's future. My dad came home to make sure I did the application for the examination correctly. He especially hoped that I would become a teacher. But he respected all my decisions. In the end, I was admitted to study at Sichuan International Studies University. My parents were very happy for me. This was my first step to achieving my dream to become a teacher.

Why did I choose English as my major? The main reason is that I regard language as a skill. And I hope to use this skill to develop my potential. We live in an era of globalization. And language is a critical bridge to link different cultures and economies around the world. I also plan to minor in management. I must confess that management is what I am good at. I believe that, with language and management, I should not have difficulty finding a job after my graduation.

And now as a freshman in the university, I will try my best to overcome all the difficulties along the way. I will learn to face the reality of college life. I will work hard to reach my original goals. I will join various campus activities to use and improve my social abilities and develop my language proficiency. The future is waiting for those who are prepared for it.

And I consider myself very lucky to have met a new friend and mentor, Steve Ling, Mary Pu's American friend. He talked to us using the internet during my final days at high school. I would never forget what he said to me, "Being a girl or being shy is not a good reason to prevent you from facing life's problems. Develop your confidence and always try your very best."

I am lucky to have met Steve Ling, and with WeChat, I hope to work with him during my four years in the university. The future is waiting for those who are prepared for it. Here I come.

PART THIRTEEN:
ON MY WAY TO BECOMING A LAWYER
By Zoey Tianfeng Zuo

My name is Tianfeng Zuo, an eighteen-year-old girl from Qianjiang, a small town in the southeast of Chongqing, which is famous for its hot pot. You can also call me by my English name, Zoey. It might prove useful one day in my future.

Because of my parents' work, away from our hometown of Qianjiang, I grew up and finished elementary school in Hangzhou, the capital city of Zhejiang Province, a bustling area of eastern China. I considered myself very lucky because I began to study English in grade three.

In my primary school, we had advanced teaching tools, which helped us learn better and gain more. Besides, we had many opportunities to relax ourselves and cultivate our interests. We also had eventful weekends and holidays, like visiting museums and zoos with friends. All these activities contributed to acquiring knowledge that we couldn't get from books. I believe we can learn from books and also from experiences.

At the age of twelve, I had no choice but to return to Qianjiang for my junior school. I found that everything there was different from Hangzhou. Instead of broad plains, my hometown was surrounded by many beautiful mountains. However, this also resulted in backward transportation and economy. There were few amusement facilities. Worse still, the schools couldn't provide us students with a high-level teaching team like the teachers I had in the city of Hangzhou.

Let us be honest, city students do have better teachers than those of us living in rural China. Take my English learning for example. I had learned English for three years before I returned to my hometown in rural China, and the students here were just beginning to study English; consequently, I have a stronger foundation than them. But because of my new English teacher's poor accent and the lack of practice, my oral English became worse and worse. The parents and teachers focused primarily on acquiring knowledge and lost sight of the importance of students' interests. I considered the education I received as exam oriented. I am willing to admit that this helps me develop the spirit of studying hard, which is beneficial for my future work. But I do feel something is missing in my Chinese education.

Great changes have taken place in my hometown since the implementation of the rural revitalization strategy and the targeted poverty alleviation policy. Many poor families have gotten effective help from the local government and have improved their life greatly. Many old houses are replaced by many tall new buildings or high-risers and shopping malls, which have brought great convenience to our life. Furthermore, schools are now equipped with advanced teaching facilities. I'm glad to witness these changes, and I also hope, one day, I can contribute to the construction of my hometown.

Everyone will encounter helpful teachers in his or her life, and I am no exception. Fortunately, I met two unforgettable teachers who mean a lot to me in my high school. One was my English teacher. I was lucky to have met him. He was always like an English gentleman and treated me like his daughter. What impressed me most about what he taught me was to believe in myself. It was his encouragement that helped me make great progress in my whole high school study.

Another is my head teacher. He is a geography teacher and has unique teaching methods, which helped me build my interest in this subject. What's more, he is also my life mentor. He raised me up when I was going through a rough time of falling out of the best class in my grade to an ordinary class because I didn't adapt to high school life at the beginning. With his help, I began to cheer up and do better in many ways. I'm really grateful to them for giving me a hand when I was confused.

Now I am starting my college life in the Southwest University of Political Science and Law (SWUPL) through the college entrance examination, which could determine my fate. And my major is law, and I want to be a lawyer because, in my eyes, a lawyer is a symbol of justice and sagacity. Besides, I want to help innocent people accused of crimes they did not commit and made the scapegoats while the criminals go free. But without action, a dream will always be a dream. Only by taking actions can a dream come true.

As for me, I'll study hard to have a good command of Chinese and professional knowledge, which are vital to an effective lawyer. I'm on my way to achieving my dream.

PART FOURTEEN:
KEEP LEARNING. DON'T SETTLE.
By Jake Chen

On October 24, 1991, I was born in Liujiang Village, Jinjiang City, Fujian Province. My hometown is famous for the many overseas Chinese, many from the Philippines. We have a spectacular coastline. Many overseas Chinese have benefited *sangzi* ("hometown" in Chinese) when they have a successful career in a foreign country. Over time, China has developed more rapidly than the Philippines and other countries.

My parents were primary school teachers in the countryside. They had devoted themselves to this career and cultivated many flowers of the motherland. Perhaps because my parents were teachers, I was very lucky to receive a lot of extra care in primary school. After entering junior high school, for me, the learning difficulty increased sharply. Coupled with the rebellious period, my academic performance fell significantly. In fact, my parents had maintained close contact with my junior middle school teachers. I had also received a lot of extra "care," but my academic performance remained somewhere in the middle and failed to make a big improvement. The high school entrance examination taught and touched me a lot. I still remember that after I missed Qiaosheng Middle School. My father said that he wanted me to enter this school. He said, "This is the middle school you like." After entering the secondary standard middle school, I did not improve significantly. I blamed it on a poor studying habit.

In high school, like many male classmates, I liked physical education, which made me happy. It was study and study from morn till night, seven days a week, without much time to do anything for fun. I had experienced the college entrance examination twice. I did not do well the first time. Then I chose to go to YangZheng Jiahui School to repeat my studies. During the second time, my teacher and the exercises given by the school helped me a lot. My father often sent me carefully stewed nutrients or special food on weekends.

I had problems with science in my Gaokao. I preferred nonscience subjects. But I did like physics a lot. I did not have good time management. I did not have strong willpower, and I was not confident in myself and my studies.

I would say I did not perform well in my second Gaokao. I talked to my uncle, a leader in a securities firm in Xiamen, a city in Fujian Province. He introduced me to Xiamen University Tan Kah Kee College because this school has many resources to help me get a good college education.

My parents were very supportive, and so I went to TKK College, a four-year college for my undergraduate studies. I liked the school because the teachers were there to help you achieve your dream. I liked the students; many were very flexible and sociable.

I enrolled in the Current Events class taught in English by a visiting professor from America. Steve Ling became my teacher, mentor, and friend. After a week or so, he told me to sit in front of his class because he suspected I had a problem focusing or concentrating in his class. So he suggested for me to sit in front in the first row so I could focus on his teaching. I tried very hard, and I did learn to improve my English.

Steve is a proactive person. His experiences from growing up in a farm to becoming a college professor, from Southeast Asia to the USA, inspire me. Be flexible, work hard, and I can change my fate to be anyone I want to be. He is a *doer*, not a *talker*.

He wanted us to call him Steve. After he returned to America, Steve and I would work together to design the covers of his books. We did them all via the internet. I designed the cover for *This Is China*, and I introduced the Chinese character "door" on the cover to show that this book is a door to understanding modern China. I also designed the cover for his second book about China called *Prodigal Son*; it was Steve's first novel or fiction about a rich college student in modern China. And for his most recent book, Bonsai Kids, about the children of the one-child policy in China (1980–2016), Steve insisted to use two photos—one of a classroom of young teenagers, the other of me speaking with a microphone to a class of young adults.

He went from a teacher to a mentor to a friend. After he returned home to America, he gave my parents his piano because they loved music. My father could play the piano, and my mother could sing. It was a perfect gift to us. And I would play my favorite harmonica. Steve jokingly suggested we should travel around the country and perform as a family trio.

After TKK College, I was hoping to study at Shenzhen University. Steve and I visited the Shenzhen campus. I have a good friend who works and lives in Shenzhen. Also, it was for a girl I like in TKK. Shenzhen became famous because Deng Xiaoping transformed that village and called it a special economic zone, and now it has become one of the busiest economic centers in modern China. It is also the headquarters of many important tech companies in the country today. I did take the graduate exam, and I was ranked twenty-second. The school could only take twenty-one students. Steve jokingly told me to wait because something could happen to a student, death or accident or anything. But I could not wait to enter a graduate school, so I returned home to Fujian Province and applied to study at Minnan Normal University (MNNU), located in my hometown. I thought of data mining, but fate would intervene, and I started studying information security in 2015. At the time, the central government in Beijing was beginning to take and treat information security very seriously. I had to thank my mother for encouraging me to pursue an advanced degree after TKK College.

Sadly, before I graduated from MNNU, my father collapsed one day while he was in his classroom. My father was always there for me, was always worried about my education and future, and often told me to focus on my study and my job.

It was at MNNU that I started to take part in CTF competitions. According to Cybertalents.com,

> CTF stands for **Capture The Flag**, This is a type of cybersecurity competitions or games with a purpose to locate a particular piece of text called a flag that may be on the server or behind a web page. Capture The Flag (CTF) competition is simulating the real world scenarios of hacking a remote site or exploiting a vulnerability on a specific application.

> A **capture the flag** (CTF) contest is a special kind of cybersecurity competition designed to challenge its participants to solve computer security problems and/ or capture and defend computer systems. Typically, these competitions are team-based and attract a diverse range of participants, including students, enthusiasts and professionals.

I would say the CTF contest was important to those of us interested in doing more research in cybersecurity. I did not consider myself a good player and did not prepare well for an information security job. As a graduate student, my main target was to write papers. And by the beginning of my final postgraduate studies, I had to find a job. I failed a few times trying to find a programmer's job. My uncle introduced me to Safedog, and because of him, I got a chance for an interview with them. Fortunately, the leader of the cybersecurity lab gave me the materials related to the new technology to study. After a week's study and preparation, I was lucky to get the opportunity to work at Safedog.

Right now, I am the leader of the new information security tech lab. My job is related to the research of cybersecurity. I am the manager of this new department. Because colleagues come and go, I work hard, and I was rewarded with the new opportunity to lead a new department. It's not that I am better than others, but the company do keep and promote those of us *steady workers* inside the company.

My company produces professional products to help the customer protect their hosts (not only private cloud but also public cloud or hybrid cloud), container security, APP security, and so on. My department is Haiqing Lab; our work is related to AI work for cybersecurity, cloud native security, vulnerability research and operation, and virus research and operation.

I am very lucky to work with a great team of people, including my boss and the vice CEO, with rules or ways to improve our efficiency, like weekly meetings, and to best implement the company-wide objectives. It is critical that we must all have a clear vision to align with to achieve success for our company (objective and key results [OKR] schedule management).

For me now, life is like a trip with endless learning. And our chief technology office (CTO) makes it clear that, as a manager, one must set the goals and deadlines for workers. It is my responsibility to do better than yesterday and to lead my soldiers and myself to achieve the goals of our company. I believe I know what is required of me and my job. I had completed two Amoy marathons and five half-marathons. These experiences taught me how to prepare and face the challenges in my life and my work.

I just became a father, and I am sure my baby will teach me how to be a better man and a father. It means more challenges and responsibilities every day. We have decided to name him Xuexian. *Xue* means "learn." And *xian* means "the man who has good character, good knowledge, or good skill." I wish I can be Xuexian myself.

Keep learning. Don't settle. That is also my role in my company.

PART FIFTEEN:
LIFE GOES ON
By Martial Jicheng Yang

My Chinese name is Yang Jicheng. Jicheng is my first name, and Yang is my last name. My English name is Martial. If you watch any soccer game, I do firmly believe you know that Manchester United has a French striker named Martial. I think you guessed right. It's because of him that I got the name Martial. The 2015–16 season just arrived at Manchester United, and they played very well.

I come from Wenzhou City, Zhejiang Province, China, which is located in a small fishing village on China's long East Coast. I'm a junior now. My major is new energy science and engineering. To be exact, my direction of study is wind power generation, but the direction of my postgraduate study in the future should be the grid power generation of electrical engineering.

I grew up in a very conservative Chinese family. I have a sister seven years older than me. When I was a child, I often fought with her, but we hardly had a quarrel since I was in high school. My father is a mason, but now he should be upgraded to a small foreman. His current job is to contract small projects and find other masons to work with him. My mother takes care of us at home. She is a very competent and virtuous mother, which can be said to be a very representative Chinese mother. Therefore, she is very strict with me in my studies.

I was slapped by her when I was a child because my handwriting was not as good as she had expected, but to be honest, I didn't hate her at all. And unlike other traditional Chinese parents, she is also very concerned about my sports. I joined the soccer team when I was in second grade in primary school until I graduated from the sixth grade. I participated in five soccer competitions in the provincial level in Zhejiang Province and always won the championship.

Two people who played soccer with me are now professional players and are playing in the Chinese Football Association China League. One of them even represented our Zhejiang team and won the under-twenty football championship in the 2021 National Games.

After primary school, I entered a private middle school. My mother's uncle was the principal there. Because my grades were also good, I was exempted from most of my tuition and miscellaneous fees. In the first grade of junior middle school, I joined the school track-and-field team and became a 1,500 m and 400 m athlete. However, in the second grade of junior middle school, my mother thought that the training in the school team would greatly affect my academic performance, so I withdrew from the team and concentrated on my studies. Then in the second semester of the third grade of junior middle school, I skipped the academic level test and directly entered one of the best high schools in our city.

Since then, my learning attitude had changed greatly. Because of my self-righteousness and the intense study in junior middle school, my nerves were highly tense. Compared with my junior high school, my academic performance had plummeted. But my mother didn't beat me or scold me. She thought it was my own business and that everyone should be responsible for all the decisions they made. Failure in the college entrance examination did not make me depressed. Instead, I accepted the result calmly. In the second half of 2019, I entered a middle-ranking university in China.

In fact, there are many stories such as of fighting and falling in love. Now I think I was naive, but this is also the only way for everyone to grow up. Now looking back on the past, I lost my beloved grandmother's parents; I lost the people who loved me deeply. I lost the people I loved deeply, but all this will eventually disappear into the sea of memories in the passage of time. Therefore, we should cherish all people and things now. There is an invisible force that makes people meet and separate.

I also like rap music very much. When I was in primary school, I learned English by listening to the songs of Eminem, Tupac, Notorious B.I.G., Dr. Dre, and Lil Wayne, such as Eminem's "Lose Yourself," "Mockingbird," "Not Behind," "Love the Way You Lie," and "Without Me" and Tupac's "Dear Mama," "Life Goes On," and "California Love." I feel that when I listen to these songs, I feel vitality, especially when I feel tired, giving me strength in spirit.

I'm also preparing to take credits, raise my GPA, participate in various competitions, and get scholarships. By the way, I'm also a member of the school football team in the university. Life goes on. Better things are yet to come.

PART SIXTEEN:
AN INTERVIEW WITH ALLEN CHEN

Allen Chen is now working for the largest insurance asset management company in China as portfolio manager since completing his postgraduate studies in master of business administration at University College London (UCL). This interview was conducted online during the winter of 2021 since we could not meet face-to-face because of the pandemic.

STEPHEN LING (SL): Welcome to this interview. I like to share your personal story with readers of my new book *Bonsai Kids*. And I consider you as one of these fortunate bonsai kids. Let me begin by asking you to share with us your earliest memory of being born as the first and only son of a Chinese family. What was it like to be the only son of your parents and the only first grandson of your grandparents? What is your earliest memory of being a little emperor?

ALLEN CHEN (AC): Thanks for having me here. My earliest memory of being the only son in my family is so vague, and I had to take a look at family photo albums. And I can confidently say that I was like a bonsai kid back then. I saw many photos of me, an infant at that time, surrounded by everyone, cuddled by Mom and Dad, held by Grandpa or Auntie. And I was there, either smiling or crying, just like a baby. However, I was intrigued to see a nanny and me in quite a few photos, and I called my mom for explanations. Well, it looks like my family didn't really have time to take care of me 24/7. I was around two to three years old. My grandpa, a war veteran, was a lawyer working days and nights; my mom was just kicking off her own business; and my grandma and dad were civil servants, devoting most of their time to the country. Understandably, they hired a babysitter, maybe two of them, to take care of me, play with me, and cook for me until I was ready for kindergarten.

SL: So in retrospect, what's it like to be the only son or little emperor?

AC: I did get all the love and attention from my family and relatives. As a result, I seemed to have many hobbies. I was into painting, playing piano, chess, swimming, robots, computer, etc. Those were quite expensive hobbies to have back in the '90s, and my family supported me regardless. However, I wouldn't really call myself a little emperor. They never allowed me to buy toys without earning my right to do so. My mom would ask me to do the family chores or homework or some errands in exchange for a small toy under thirty yuan, and I had to share it with my cousins. I guess this was my first adult lesson at the age of five. I have to earn my rewards, learn to listen, and share with others. In a nutshell, I was aware of values, principles, and rules at an early age, and those have deep influences on me till today.

That being said, I now can see that my mom and dad did spend quality time with me because, in every photo out there, I was always smiling, I was not isolated, and I was given freedom to experience the world on my own with their full support. This is surely my earliest memory of being the so-called bonsai kid before schools.

SL: At what age did you start schooling, and how well did you do in primary, junior high, and high school? You were aware of "values, principles, and rules at an early age." You must be a superintelligent kid. What in your education or early exposure to your family and the world around you taught you these values, principles, and rules?

AC: I started my schooling at the age of seven and had always been one of the top students in primary, junior high, and high school. I was not forced to study overtime, and I did not even actively participate in supplementary classes during the weekends like many others did. The bottom line was that my parents would allow me to pursue my hobbies as long as I achieved relatively high grades. Teaching me the right attitude and principles is at the crux of their parenting methodologies because I was expected to follow in the footsteps of my father and grandpa in a career as a government official, making a contribution to China in the future. To achieve this, my family members led by example.

Unlike many other children in a one-child policy system, I proved to be rebellious and independent instead of being pampered and spoiled like a little emperor. It was my grandfather, a war veteran and a lawyer, who instilled virtues in me. My grandfather had an ever-present smile, a sense of justice, and a kind heart to help others. However, he often regretted not being able to see the outside world after the war and make a difference in modern China. He was the first to mold my thinking and dedication to realize the dream of making a positive impact in the world. He and my father often debated on political and economic issues at the dinner table, where I often joined and argued as well. Even at a young age, I found it comfortable convincing the elders of some of my ideas with "rigid" arguments.

My father enjoyed mentoring me on how I should behave and act while meeting with his friends and colleagues, particularly in building integrity, trust, and reputation. There was always a pile of *Journal of Chinese Leadership* on my father's desk, along with my favorite book, *The Art of War*.

On other hand, females are actually the backbone of my family. My grandma is a people person. She used to manage all the chores and finances of the family. She was dedicated to her job as a human resource director at local tax bureau where she was named the Bearer of Red Flag March 8, a national award given to outstanding women workers nationwide. Yet she was kind enough to give back to society every day. Even this year, I saw her share gifts and food to homeless or vulnerable people in the community. She's been doing this for ages.

My mother is a successful businesswoman who always asked me to excel at everything I do and set a higher standard every time I succeeded. Deeply influenced by her passion, decisiveness, toughness, and empowering leadership, I formed the foundation of my interests and curiosity in *business and professional excellence*. During a visit to her office, I was fascinated by the colored line charts displayed on the monitor and learned that it is called stock trading. Shortly after that, I started using my mom's account to trade stocks in high school. Fast-forward, now I am managing three hundred billion renminbi funds in China.

What I learned at an early age from my family was to cultivate the right habits: always striving for excellence and making positive impacts on the things and people around me. Thanks to those values, principles, and rules gained at an early age, I—once regarded as a top student in high school—was not depressed by the very poor college entrance exam result that led me to TKK College. I was able to adapt and thrive at TKK and ultimately decided to make a change—applying to study overseas.

SL: You mentioned "the very poor college entrance exam result" that led you to enroll at Xiamen University Tan Kah Kee College, a very expensive private school in mainland China. Of course, you are referring to the national college entrance examination or Gaokao (a Mandarin word that translates into "high exam"). Held annually in the People's Republic of China for as many as ten million high school students as the sole criterion or prerequisite for entrance into almost all universities at the undergraduate level, Gaokao is notorious for being one of the toughest, grueling exams in the world.

In 2012, there were shocking images of a student taking intravenous injections while preparing for the exam. And in 2014, an eighteen-year-old took his own life when he failed his Gaokao. As a Chinese yourself, do you understand why some Chinese parents prefer to send their sons and daughters overseas to pursue a high school education to prevent their children from the anguish and suffering of Gaokao in mainland China? If you have a high school son or daughter, would you do it too?

You know, there is obvious regional imbalance where students in urban areas have greater access to better educational resources than those in most rural areas in China. Do you think Gaokao is a fair way for Chinese universities to select their students? Some Western universities are trying to do away with SAT, for example. What are your thoughts on these issues?

AC: Relatively speaking, only a small number of wealthy families have the financial capacity to send their kids to high school abroad because schools usually charge higher fees on overseas students, whereas it is almost free to study at a high school in China. Also, a Chinese high school delivers much stronger science education (i.e., STEM) compared with their counterparts in Western countries. But Western schools tend to cultivate students through a variety of resources and elective courses that would benefit a person's personality and logical reasoning abilities. Both education systems have pros and cons. It is up to the parents to decide whether they have the ability and willingness to send their kids aboard.

So what would I do? It depends. Let's say I will have enough money to send my kids abroad. So the question is whether it is good for them. For example, my wife has been an elite student throughout her life, ranking top 1 percent since primary school. She loves academic challenges and exams. She enjoys it a lot and is pretty good at it. So she's fine with Gaokao in China and was even thrilled at taking them. I am not like her. I hated endless exams with predetermined answers. I sometimes even challenged the questions and interviewers. Therefore, I guess it really depends on whether my kids have enough intellectual capacity to cope with the highly competitive Gaokao and whether they have a certain level of interests/passion in pursuing this academic route. For university education, I'd definitely send them abroad.

Regarding fairness in Gaokao, I'd say it's a brilliant design we inherited from the ancient Chinese, the civil service exam system—a system of testing designed to select the most studious and learned candidates for appointment as bureaucrats in the Chinese government. This system governed who would join the bureaucracy between 650 CE and 1905, making it the world's longest-lasting meritocracy. Either way, it is probably impossible to completely level the playing field for everyone for any country.

Yes, there's still greater imbalance between students in Beijing (the capital of China) and people in some rural areas. For example, only top-tier students from Fujian would get a chance to enroll in Peking University, while students with lesser capacity would find it easy to enroll simply because they live in Beijing. But China's Gaokao, in general, does give ordinary people *a chance* to change their life for good. It also eliminates corruption to some degree despite a few reported cases. As we know, wealthy and influential American families also tried to cheat in SAT. So it's nothing new.

Another key factor to consider is the prevailing online study where students nowadays can get access to high-quality teaching resources outside their hometown. Adults can now try to earn advanced online degrees from top universities, such as Columbia, Harvard, Chicago Booth, or HKUST, after working for a couple of years. For undergraduate studies, I still believe that in-person lecturing is crucial.

SL: You said previously, "I was able to adapt and thrive at TKK and ultimately decided to make a change—applying to study overseas." Here is a simple question for you. Your wealthy parents were able to enroll you at Xiamen University Tan Kah Kee College, one of the best but most expensive private colleges in mainland China. What do you mean by your ability to adapt and thrive at TKK, and why did you make the radical decision to study abroad?

AC: Like many other kids in my generation, I was educated under the typical Chinese educational system, attending public schools, having extra lectures, and studying twelve hours a day. The priority on studying for the school exams, however, did not prevent me from pursuing other activities, like traveling, drawing, and playing sports and guitar. I was consistently ranked top 1 percent throughout my high school years and was expected to achieve good results in the national college entrance exam. My family and friends expected me to enroll in top schools like Peking Uni, Tsinghua Uni, or at least Xiamen Uni.

However, I failed. I was too nervous and anxious before the exams, and my mind was blank during the exams because there was so much at stake, so much hope, and so much expectations. I simply could not handle the pressure.

After receiving the results, which were roughly 40 percent of what was expected out of my normal performance, I was in shock for a couple of weeks. I did not hang out with my classmates, and I did not even try to play video games. I needed to decide whether to retake my high school final year. It was tough for me because of the high intensity and pressure. I left it up to my parents to decide my fate, my college destination, and "my future." They chose environmental science engineering (ESE) at TKK, which they thought would provide me with a fast track to Xiamen Uni for postgraduate studies. Therefore, I did not choose TKK or the major. It was my family who believed that this degree would promise me a decent career path in the future.

Since I did not want to retake my final year in high school either, I had to leave all the pressure and disappointment of my exam failure behind, and I decided to attend TKK after all. *To my great surprise, university is society in miniature, and the campus life was surely exciting for me as a freshman.* I was the lead waltz dancer at the freshmen welcome ceremony, a journalist in my department, and also an active member of many student societies.

Living alone far away from home might be difficult for some little emperors, but for me, it was an opportunity to embrace a new life, an independent one. I decided to travel the unknown road—taking a transfer exam and switching to finance and banking. I was soon elected class president and won first-class scholarship with an above average 90 percent grade, ranking no. 1 in the Finance Department after a semester. I found no difficulty in organizing several events, leading classmates on the campus life with excellent grades. Apart from starting my own stock investment, my mother has decided to let me become an external consultant to three of my mother's companies while doing a summer internship. I was then expected to follow a typical finance student career path—completing a distinct degree and then pursuing a job at a bank or applying for a master's degree.

Fortunately, someone helped me out of my muddle. Prof. Wu Kelong, the dean of the Management Department who earned a MBA degree in the USA, was my lecturer in Principles of Management and Art of Leadership, in which I scored 96 percent and 99 percent respectively. He showed me what makes a good leader, an excellent businessman, and more importantly a man who loves his work and lives with a vision. Guiding me through MBA education, management experiences in Fortune 500 companies, his teaching experience, and the importance of EQ, he believed I have the potential to be an effective leader and encouraged me to explore the world at an early age.

One night I picked up my guitar and sat by the lake, playing some music and calculating the opportunity cost of dropping out at TKK and studying abroad. Two days later, I filed a dropout application after I drafted a ten-year plan—getting an undergraduate degree in Europe for three years, working for two years, applying for a two-year full-time MBA, and finally joining consulting or other business start-ups for a few years before building my own business start-up.

Setting aside the plan, I still needed to take the IELTS and apply for universities in the UK. At the time, my family disagreed with my decision but pleased with a grown-up child who could make his own call. If you recall, I didn't make any choices on my own after the college entrance exam. It was probably the first time for me to really go against the will of my parents and go all out.

But I had become so convinced that I gotta study overseas, and I took the IELTS and applied for universities in the UK. Luckily, I passed the language exam and got accepted by a few British universities. *Just like that, my own adventure of life began.*

After I accepted the offer for an economics degree at the University of Bath at UK, I had to finish my second year of studies at TKK. In that semester, I noticed that many students who are keen on studying abroad encountered great difficulty studying English and applying to study abroad. Taking advantage of the opportunity, I drafted a business start-up plan for a nonprofit organization and recruited six students from different departments, including students from accounting, finance, English, economics, and computer science. We set up an online forum, did some on-campus marketing, reached out for sponsors, and invited lecturers to be advisers. The website served as the information exchange center for students in China. More than a thousand registered at the time, and I had the opportunity to know the students who were eager to expand their horizon abroad and had a big dream for the future.

Unfortunately, it would be extremely hard to manage the organization every day while studying full time in the UK. I had to shut down the website. What matters the most is that my team members were inspired by my visions and ideas as we learned and grew together along the way. This was different from the way their parents had always told them, and they decided to discover the future for themselves, going to the UK or the USA for a master's degree, becoming a teacher or hotel management trainee, doing things they actually love, and thriving along the way. For me, I realized that I can motivate my peers and inspire them to excel in a positive way. *In late 2011, with all the excitement, I landed in London.*

SL: You received an offer for an economics degree at the University of Bath at the UK and landed in London in 2011. You, more or less, finished the first two years of your undergraduate degree in China and the final the years in the UK. A Chinese student new in the UK told me an interesting story of what happened to him when he tried to find a place to live while going to school in the UK. The landlady had said to him that for him to sign the housing contract, he would have to agree to "not speak another word of Chinese in her house." From China to UK, how difficult was your adjustment to life in a whole different milieu socially, culturally, and academically? And I remember you sent me a photo—a before-and-after photo of how you cut your own hair. What was that all about?

AC: First and foremost, I made the decision to study abroad, so I shall get myself prepared to face the challenges ahead. Before I went to London, I had around three months of preparation. I tried everything I could at that time—researching British history, local cultures, dos and don'ts, lifestyle, coffee shops, bank locations, mobile phone retailers, grocery shops, local attractions, dangerous areas, you name it. I also tried to hone my language ability by talking with various foreign teachers in Xiamen and online. Then I started reading study materials and newspapers in English. For example, I would go through *Financial Times*, the *Economist*, the *Wall Street Journal*, *Washington Post*, economics textbooks, and academic papers. In a nutshell, I didn't just chill and wait for my flight. I worked even harder. Such attitude had laid the foundation for me to adapt to a new life in the UK.

Academically, I had no trouble at all. Simply put, I studied hard because studying in the UK was my choice, and I had to hold myself accountable for my decision. While studying economics helps me understand the world in which I live and work, living in the real world, unlike the one I came from, is a very different story. Unlike the typical Chinese education system, whether you can succeed in the UK requires you to be disciplined and take initiative to study yourself. For instance, attendance at lectures are not compulsory, and you might have several optional modules to choose from. One might end up attending zero lectures a year but scoring unexpectedly high in the exams based on talents and diligence in the library. Others might simply fail the courses and waste one more year retaking the courses. The situation varies from student to student.

For international students, language ability is a prerequisite if one wants to excel in an English-speaking environment. Mastering the English language is not required to complete a degree, but proficiency in it would boost study efficiency and productivity. It's common to see Chinese students "herding" in lecture halls, and they would never go out to a party or pub whatsoever. This is totally fine if they are aiming solely at a degree or a diploma. I would ask a simple question: why are we in the university in the first place? Is it worth our sacrifices for a piece of paper? Will a diploma become the sole factor in determining my future career pursuit? The answers will vary from person to person.

Personally speaking, the biggest challenge for me was to be ready to make necessary adjustments to a new *culture* before I left China. Some things come naturally; some don't. When things go wrong, all of us naturally feel disappointed and frustrated. I might get stunned and deeply upset. Some experiences might have a negative impact on me, especially when I am alone in a new culture. Mental preparation might not be enough. At times, it might be better to go with the flow.

After I landed in London, I proactively reached out to flatmates, classmates, student ambassadors, lecturers, local people (neighbors) and talked to them. Having rich and interactive conversations with various people gave me fresh and different perspectives on things. I am fortunate enough to know many kindhearted people who are willing to help others and to share stories. They offered me support and advice that I could never forget. Although I was always into some unfamiliar situations in the early months after my arrival, I got help when needed. I appreciate that till today.

During term breaks, I traveled to some European countries, starting with Barcelona when Spain was experiencing economic downturns and strikes. Despite the chaos, I met an ordinary coffee shop owner, and we discussed world politics, economy, and inequality. He taught me that actions are worth more than a thousand words. I was impressed by this knowledgeable man and even learned some basic Spanish from him. Apart from studying and traveling, I led teams to represent the University of Bath for business challenge competitions in the UK. It was an honor for me to work with students from diverse backgrounds, but I did learn a great deal from their cultures and personalities.

In the meantime, I enjoy sharing my knowledge with my British, European, and Japanese friends and discuss the economy, investments, and business opportunities in the world nowadays. How did I manage to do that? *Master English.*

I studied economics, but I am also a part-time translator. Mandarin is gaining its momentum, but mastering English would give you unparalleled advantage over others, though the bottom line is that you have to be proactive and open-minded when interacting with people from various backgrounds. Oh, and yes, I did start to cut my own hair in the UK. Nothing in particular, just one of many new things I started doing since going abroad.

In all, it was a three-year undergrad in the UK, but I took a gap year, working full time in London after my second year.

SL: You said, "In all, it was a three-year undergrad in the UK, but I took a gap year, working full time in London after my second year."

I read somewhere that "students who take gap years typically achieve a growth in maturity and are better prepared to benefit from higher education or decide the form of education they wish to pursue." Also, "Studies indicate that students who take a gap year perform better academically than those who do not, however, many parents worry that their children will defer continuation of their education."

Did you consult the gap year with your parents back home in China? What is your response to the quotes I am sharing with you, particularly with references to growth in maturity and performing better academically? It seems obvious to me you were not in a hurry to graduate but chose a gap year. Why? And did you accomplish what you anticipated during your internship?

AC: No, I did not consult with my parents beforehand. I talked with the lecturers, alumni, and career tutor at university. But I did inform and share my experiences with my parents regularly.

In my second year at the University of Bath, my gut feelings told me that *I have to take full advantage of studying abroad and to test myself in the real business world as I started to look for a job in central London*, an economic powerhouse and the best place for me to work in a truly international and competitive business environment. After roughly thirty-one interviews, if I remember correctly, I got a few offers. Some employers are based in Bath, some are based in Edinburgh, and some are located in London. In the end, I went to work for a top market research consultancy near the famous City Hall and Tower Bridge in central London. As an intern, I worked hard on the task at hand and learned to design programs that benefit those tasks, and I started gaining credibility and recognition within the team. As I frequently produced results beyond expectations, I began to receive invitations to work on bigger accounts, create more effective tools, and manage ad hoc projects. Consequently, I was often invited by colleagues to discuss how we can improve a project's efficiency and profitability. It was this kind of momentum that ultimately led me to make an impact on the company.

After being introduced to the entire UK branch by the head of the training department, I started to create an Excel manual that is tailored for our day-to-day tasks. To ensure that everyone can use and update the manual in the future without my presence, I added detailed instructions, and we set up a few training sessions for me to mentor fellow interns, graduates, project managers, and even directors. More importantly, those who attended the training sessions are committed to train their colleagues. I will never forget the smile on a manager's face when he told me that an Excel trick I taught him has forever changed a task he had been doing for years. When I received the most nominations and votes for the Employee Success Award, I finally realized that my colleagues had a great amount of respect for me, and they trusted me.

My gap year experience had surely exceeded my expectation. What I am most proud of is an idea that I represent—the possibility of achieving the impossible. After the team took my advice on how to improve the internship scheme, they decided to put up a poster of my experience and achievements. In late 2017, three years after my gap year, I received a LinkedIn message from a graduate whom I had never met. He told me that looking at my poster really gave him the courage and motivation to work harder because I was modeling for them the things they want to see and follow. It was one of the important moments in my life because I realized that the legacy I left behind is not just some tools or manuals but also a culture that fosters the greatness in people.

Living in London is not just about working hard. Apart from networking with elite bankers in the city, I also made friends with several visiting professors and PhDs in science. While they are impressed by my personality, experience, and long-term career plan, I found it very inspiring and fascinating to talk to those future Chinese pioneer scientists and learned about the science and the way they perceive science, society, government, and the world as a whole. Some of them and my classmates in China often tell me that they believe in me and will join my business start-up in the future. Many have great courses, and many have the capacity to pull it off.

For me, the trust from my colleagues and friends is simply something money cannot buy. I believe that we still have quite a lot of students in China who "failed" at their university entrance exam and believed that it's the end of their career pursuit. I can confidently tell them that *it's not.* After networking with the brightest Oxford/Cambridge students or elite investment bankers or well-rounded consultants, I realized that they're no smarter than most of us. But they all worked extremely hard, and they're willing to sacrifice their personal leisure to thrive in their pursuit. That's something we called EQ or emotional intelligence.

In June 2015, I accepted a summer internship offer at a hedge fund in central London because I was so eager to see what the top financial world really looks like, not the sell-side investment bank but the famous moneymaking machine—hedge fund. On one hand, I finally got a chance to apply the economic or finance theories that I learned at school, something like option pricing, arbitrage trading, and trading tactics. I got a few thousands, and they got a billion. But as you probably know, hedge fund managers tend to be millionaires, and they are famous for being cunning, cold-blooded, and money driven. They celebrate their success in short-selling stocks while Greece was suffering from a debt crisis, and they simply robbed hundreds of thousands of dollars from others. And the next day, my boss simply texted me and said that he's on his private jet for a vacation because they've "killed" someone in the market and made a fortune. Well, I guess that's pretty much all I used to talk about hedge funds then.

In July 2015, I finally received my degree in economics at the University of Bath. It's been six years. Though I wasn't studying all the time, dropping out in China and taking a gap year working in

London surely add something to my résumé and, more importantly, bring more reflections on myself. Once again, I applied to numerous firms in London and had a dozen interviews. Despite having multiple offers (and rejections, of course) from firms in London, I can't resist the temptation of accepting the one from the largest asset management firm in Wall Street in the United States. And I said yes without hesitation. Why? *Some people resign themselves to do things they don't like and figure success or enjoyment just isn't in their cards. As for me, I go with my passion and ambition, which make study or work easier and success more likely and enjoyable. I keep an ambition to excel and eagerness for challenges and a flexibility of mind.* Am I impressed by the fact that I'm going to work in Wall Street? Not really because I know what I want to do with my life, and that is just a great opportunity for me to gain insights into the top financial world and learn about US culture.

The experiences in Europe and the United States ultimately made me reflect on my upbringing, family ties, and career aspiration. Finally, I decided to go back to my motherland, China.

SL: You said, "Am I impressed by the fact that I'm going to work in Wall Street? Not really because I know what I want to do with my life, and that is just a great opportunity for me to gain insights into the top financial world and learn about US culture." With all your successes in London, you continue to explore the financial world, and you finally got your wish—to work in Wall Street.

Why is Wall Street so important to you or your résumé? What did you learn about the American culture and that of Wall Street? And are you happy and satisfied where you are today, working in your own motherland, mainland China? What is your China dream, if you have one?

AC: For anyone who studies economics, finance, or politics, it is crucial that he or she understands the history and development of world economies, especially the United Kingdom, the United

States, and China. After WWII, the United States has emerged as the world's greatest nation, and its success relies heavily on the supreme economic power, which is largely driven by its financial market and participants. Wall Street is literally a street located in New York City—at the southern end of Manhattan, to be precise. But figuratively, Wall Street is much more, a synonym for the financial industry and the firms within it. The term *Wall Street* means "business—the investment business—and the interests, motivations, and attitudes of its players." To get a decent front-office job in Wall Street is considered to be both challenging and prestigious because Wall Street deeply influences the US politics and economy, hence the world.

Having work experience at the largest investment management firm in the world, BlackRock, in New York does polish my résumé to some extent. However, it is the American culture and that of Wall Street that ultimately shape my career path and life choices. Both America and Britain have some very different culture practices. However, the history of America and Britain is intertwined, which is why a lot of similarities also occur. American culture is more open-minded and entrepreneurial than the British one. And the American dream is advocated everywhere you go. Another difference is in the sense of humor. The British are famous for their sarcastic sense of humor, while the Americans have a straight sense of humor. The culture of Wall Street, on the other hand, is just the same as the culture of financial center in London—smartness, elitism, hard work, profit, and greed.

So after I had some hands-on experience on the culture of Wall Street, namely, fulfilling my "dream," I learned that it is not what I really want. *It was time for a change. After seven years of studying and working abroad, I decided to return to my motherland, China.*

To tell you the truth, I am not satisfied with my current job in China. I'm closer to my family, and I am a happy married man now with a beautiful wife. However, my career development has stalled because I chose to work for a state-owned enterprise, although the employer is the largest institutional investor in China, ranked no. thirty-eight worldwide and no. one in China regarding its asset under management. And I'm responsible for investing and management of assets (i.e., bonds, stocks) with RMB 30 billion in asset under management.

But I'm actually at the lowest point of my career in terms of aspiration and motivation. The culture here does not fit with my personality, personal drive, skill sets, and career aspiration. Although senior leaders at the firm told me that I've been doing a great job, I found *zero* motivation and willingness to stay any longer. The job is not challenging at all despite its prestige and requires zero learning/development. It does not make a difference if you add value to the job. As long as you don't make mistakes, you can earn your basic salary. China is currently competing with the United States on many facets. I have to be rational and stay calm, waiting for the right opportunity to appear.

Nope, I don't have a China dream. I believe the definition varies depending on whom you ask. I'd say my dream is to have a happy family (which I have) and a fulfilling career that maximizes my skill sets and potential. Ideally, I'd achieve financial independence and have enough free time to explore the world and interact with many more people from different backgrounds (namely, getting to know more about the world).

CHAPTER THIRTY-SIX

China is changing as fast as a chameleon as it continues to define and redefine its role while facing the many challenges from within and without today in the twenty-first century. What is China? Who is China in the modern world? It is impossible to write about every socioeconomic, cultural, or political issue facing the nation now or, for that matter, the whole new generation of the bonsai kids. However, there are certain issues that are more critical or urgent than others in my view as an American or someone who had the privilege to spend seven years as a visiting professor in China.

Should the bonsai kids be concerned that the Chinese Communist Party (CCP) is asking or insisting that all the billionaires give back some of their enormous wealth to help the less fortunate or those who, for various reasons, were left behind during the period of unprecedented economic boom in China?

Granted, it is true that the recent decades of the relentless pursuit of economic growth (especially since the economic reforms and opening up of the early 1980s) have created more billionaires than the United States of America. Through the intensive and massive nationwide *poverty alleviation programs,* China can boast to the world that they have successfully lifted about eight hundred million people (the population of the USA is slightly over three hundred million) out of poverty, though another six hundred million are living on $150 a month.

Honestly? I spent seven eventful years in China as a visiting professor
and realized one could live very cheaply in China since most of
the "poor" people are living in remote rural areas, where they are
able to raise some animals and grow different vegetables to feed
themselves. And for this reason, many so-called migrant workers
choose to leave their rural homes to work in China's major cities to
make a good living, leaving their children behind to be raised by
their grandparents and occasionally, during major national holidays,
returning home to focus on building their dream houses in many
rural areas across China. Urbanites are not allowed to own land or
build their own houses. Only those living in rural areas, as part of
the land reforms in China and the Chinese *hukou* system, are given
lands for cultivation and also to build their own houses.

A house in urban areas is beyond the reach of the average Chinese.
Majority, therefore, dwell in cagelike apartments across China. Many
of these migrant workers are returning home to these rural areas
with lots of money they have worked for and saved and are now
building their "mansions" in rural China. I saw quite a few of them
while visiting my students in rural areas. These gigantic mansions
with tall iron fencing and gates (like one you might see in wealthy
Hollywood in the USA) with huge TV screens and gaudy crystal
chandeliers seem so out of place in rural China. And some of these
houses, many now owned by migrant workers, might remain vacant
while the occupants return to work in cities in China.

In this context, should the bonsai kids be concerned that Pres. Xi
Jinping is trying to restructure the Chinese society by cracking down
on the newly minted superrich to redistribute the enormous wealth
more evenly among the 1.4 billion people in modern China? Should
the bonsai kids be concerned with their beloved President Xi in
his pursuit of "common prosperity," meaning regulating excessive
incomes or encouraging people or enterprises with high income to
return more to the Chinese society? Should they be concerned with

their beloved president's new attempt to reshape the Chinese society to achieve socialism with Chinese characteristics?

And this new pursuit of better income equality, to the world, seems like a self-preservation rationale. Is it? Watch YouTube, and there are videos after videos showing President Xi caring about and visiting the downtrodden and those left behind during China's economic boom in many remote areas across China, and one might understand his new pursuit of common prosperity or his China dream or socialism with Chinese characteristics. It has been his goal from the start of his presidency, now gaining more momentum. In a strange way, why not? Because China's economic growth has outpaced that of any major economy on this planet within the past four decades or so.

China is proud to show the world its forward-thinking government that cares about its citizens. And the government is going beyond the economy, now striving to limit video gaming hours for minors. As bonsai kids, are you concerned that the government is working hard to stamp out a fan culture that encourages its youth to blindly idolize their celebrities? Or do you agree with the voice of a female nineteen-year-old college student when she said, "Common prosperity means that everybody can live a high-quality life. People will live a healthier life, be better behaved, have a happier mood and will be more likely to pursue and realize their dreams."

CHAPTER THIRTY-SEVEN

As the new generation of bonsai kids, are you concerned that some of your contemporaries are "lying flat" because they are tired of the competitive world around them, exhausted, and willing to give up hope about their lives and their future? It seems this "lying flat" disease is affecting the youth of China, South Korea, and Japan.

Many young people across China want out of the fierce competition for college and jobs, now happily following a new way of thinking called *tang ping* or "lying flat." Someone came up with the idea that bonsai kids should chase after a simple life instead of acquisition of an apartment, expensive wedding, and traditional family values. Fuck them! Instead, just lie flat and live a simple life. Avoid the demanding, grueling work culture, especially in high-tech companies or start-ups demanding you to sacrifice your lives for progress and profits at your expense. But the government suggests for young people to work hard for a better future. Whose thinking is more important? The government or your own?

Yes, many young people in China and across East Asia are eschewing material possessions, exhausted by working hard for limited rewards, some giving up on marriage and home ownership. (No one will marry you unless you own an apartment.) Many are asking themselves, *Why am I working so hard? For what?* They are burned out. Forget the conventional rites of passage, like owning a house, getting married, and having children to please your parents.

So many of them just want to lie flat. So the *tang ping* lifestyle is starting to resonate with many young people today. So what does a *tang ping* lifestyle look like? In the words of one manifesto, "I will not marry, buy a house or have children, I will not buy a bag or wear a watch. I will slack off at work . . . I am a blunt sword to boycott consumerism."

A record 9.09 million young people graduated from university in 2021, and the pressures awaiting them are high. Many bemoan intense work schedules or the excessive work culture known as "996" (working from nine to nine for six days a week), especially if they work for major tech firms or white-collar jobs. Essentially, at times, they compete with their fellow workers or colleagues, some feeling compelled to do so just to keep up with the Joneses, so much so that, recently, China's top court accused companies of violating labor rules.

In Japan, wives can sue a company because their husbands have died from *karoshi* (working to death) or *karo-jisatsu* (suicide by overwork). *Karoshi* or *karo-jisatsu* is one of the consequences of working very long hours, leading to an employee's deteriorating health and death. And because of so many deaths of young professionals in Japan, the government has to pass laws to tell them when to close their office. The tragedy is many think that, to keep their jobs, they must work harder and longer for their companies, so much so that some Japanese women are afraid to get married or have babies because some companies prefer someone who are devoted 120 percent to their jobs.

Worse, the rising cost of owning an apartment adds to the pressure. And many are opting out of dating, marriage, and children. In South Korea, it is called *sampo* or "give up three," describing a new generation of those who are giving up dating, marriage, and children. Now it is the *opo* or "give up five" generation, giving up home ownership and interpersonal relationships in addition to *sampo*.

In Japan, young people are frustrated with economic stagnation for years. The *satori sedai* or "resignation generation" refers to those embracing pessimistic attitudes about the future or lacking material desires. And in a recent survey, many of them associate themselves with the *satori* generation, less materialistic and less interested in consumption, blaming their outlook on economic stagnation since its asset bubble burst in early 1990s. They will do what is expected of them, not more.

So what does the future look like? Shifting demographics should be a concern for many young people across East Asia—China, Japan, and South Korea. For example, China is now encouraging more couples to have three children to arrest a demographic crisis, with its population growing at its slowest rate in decades. South Korea recorded more deaths than births for the first time last year. It is a major economic concern of these countries that there won't be enough young people to keep its economic engines running or powering its economic growth.

It could spell economic disaster if the *tang ping* mentality were to take over the minds of the young people. One can only hope many would still want to work hard for a better life and future.

CHAPTER THIRTY-EIGHT

Many foreign companies are setting up branch offices, regional headquarters, and factories in mainland China, furthering the country's rapid economic growth, the fastest in the world for the past decades. And the demand for highly talented workers or people with local and international managerial skills now exceeds supply, "driving up some of the compensation packages for top talents and managers to global levels." Should the bonsai kids be concerned with bridging China's talent gap?

Some troubling problems that the bonsai kids must face today are lack of fluency in spoken English (yes, many Chinese students can write but not speak well in English or other foreign languages), too much theoretical and not enough practical learning, limited work experiences but higher pay and rapid advancement expectation, and frequent going from job to job (with some companies reporting 10 to 30 percent annual talent turnover). Should the bonsai kids be concerned with China's educational system, relying heavily on memorization, while increasingly the business world workforce needs people with competencies in teamwork skills, leadership ability, speaking skills, and creative writing or practical experiences and softer creative and leadership skills? This is a problem as more young people are pursuing university and graduate degrees that should have equipped them with competencies required in the business world. Experienced managers are in short supply. The multinationals are facing a serious challenge of where and how to recruit the best people but also how to develop and retain them.

Sadly, the population in China is aging rapidly. Many of those forty and over are not well educated, and the pool of talent is inadequate for most companies. And those with the most talent, those in their twenties and thirties, are shrinking over time. And these bonsai kids, with improved health and higher level of educational achievement, are "often hungry for responsibility, position, and the trappings of success in order to support not only themselves but also their aging and large extended families." And one reason for the high staff turnover rates is that many will move readily between employers for a higher salary, more status, and better opportunities to rise to the top of their profession.

And so to compete economically in the world stage, the Chinese government knows it must provide better education for the bonsai kids. And the good news is some multinationals are forging links with the universities to bring about change and getting whatever skills they want as a consequence of their involvement in China's educational system. Of course, it is not easy to radically change China's "learn by rote" educational system. Many Chinese managers are behind in teamwork and creativity skills.

Here is some good news about today's bonsai kids in China. They are urban, young, and bright; many are university educated, eager to work for top domestic companies or multinationals. And they are dedicated, ambitious, and hardworking.

CHAPTER THIRTY-NINE

Maybe China could use the Amy Chuas of the world to impose parental authority on their children playing the latest computer games in the privacy of their rooms or somewhere in less-controlled or supervised computer bars and cafés located right at the doorsteps of many Chinese junior high and high schools or universities across mainland China. One could use Amy Chua and her no-nonsense, old-fashioned authoritarianism to solve China's overwhelming addiction to the computer games.

Instead of deploying the Amy Chuas of the world, China is ordering gaming companies to no longer allow children under eighteen to play online video games between Monday and Thursday and only for one hour between eight and nine in the evening on Fridays, Saturdays, Sundays, and national holidays. Also, all gaming companies must register with an antiaddiction service and put in place real-name verification to prevent young people from posing as adults. Is this the best way to combat the spiritual opium of gaming addiction? Or is this Pres. Xi Jinping's attempt to align the country's big businesses with his overarching values for the country? Some young people might think their government is being ruthless in doing this to them.

In 2019, China restricted gaming hours for teens to 1.3 hours per day. Gaming parlors are now allowed to offer services from eight to nine in the evening on Fridays, weekends, and public holidays. Young Chinese gamers are angry; so what? The government is concerned that too many hours of indulging in online games affect the normal study life and the physical and mental health of growing teenagers. And here is a simple rationale for the government's strict rule: destroying a teenager will destroy a family. To many young people, it seems a joke because you can work at sixteen, give sexual consent at fourteen, and are allowed to play games at eighteen.

As bonsai kids, are you concerned with the long-term growth of the gaming industry or its immediate revenue or that this restriction by the Chinese government will destroy the habit-forming nature of playing online games at an early age? I wrote elsewhere in this book about a TV report of migrant workers trying to visit their son at a camp for kids addicted to computer games. The boy refused to talk to his parents, essentially blaming them for neglecting him while they were away as migrant workers, trying to make some money so their only son could get a good education.

The problem is not just children of migrant workers but also children introduced to computers at an early age by their overanxious or ambitious parents. The only child must have the best of anything and everything. And many things happened to the children while they are away, living in dormitories as early as junior high school. What they do in the computer bars or cafés are beyond the reach of their parents despite many schools forbidding their students to bring a computer to school for personal use. This is China.

CHAPTER FORTY

As bonsai kids, are you worried about Pres. Xi Jinping's rhetoric about common prosperity, his endeavor to close China's wealth gap? It seems *common prosperity* has appeared sixty-five times in his speeches this year alone while sporadically the first eight years of his presidency. To outsiders or China watchers, use of certain slogans is indicative of new policy directions or changes in the making.

As bonsai kids, are you worried that the government's top economic and financial leaders are encouraging philanthropy and income distribution into the ideal olive-shaped structure, reflecting small on top and bottom and fat in the middle? Will the government achieve its egalitarian dream?

Common prosperity was first introduced by the founder of communist China, Chairman Mao Zedong, but his successor, Deng Xiaoping, shifted his focus to allowing "some people to get rich first," followed by common prosperity later. Maybe President Xi is concerned that the wealth is not trickling down to the hoi polloi fast enough, with 400 million people (a third of its 1.4 billion people) enjoying an annual household income between one hundred thousand and five hundred thousand yuan, while 600 million still live on a monthly income of one thousand yuan. Should the bonsai kids be concerned with the trap of high welfare?

Emphasis on material comfort? How to implement policies that encourage the hoi polloi to achieve wealth through hard work? President Xi wants common prosperity for all by 2035? China's modus operandi is a pilot program designed to narrow the income gap by 2025 (just around the corner), which is being introduced in Zhejiang Province on the East Coast.

CHAPTER FORTY-ONE

As the new generation of bonsai kids, are you concerned that TV stars and tech billionaires have become obvious scapegoats for public anger as China's economy slows? It seems the era of a better life is about over, thus putting increasing pressure on the Communist Party to find ways to allow and encourage the hoi polloi to achieve their dreams of a better and happier life.

Are you concerned that celebrity names are being deleted from credits of famous TV shows? "Sissy boys" or effeminate male idols are being vilified. Are you concerned that foreign textbooks are being banned and that more classes on the thinking of the leadership of President Xi Jinping are encouraged?

And filthy rich tech giants are urged to donate to philanthropy. What is wrong with that? It is President Xi's way to purge the Chinese society of moral failings, corruption, and greed, a threat to his goal of socialism with Chinese characteristics or common prosperity or the campaign to narrow the gap between the superrich and the poor and create "material and spiritual wealth."

And why not? He is against Western influences and freewheeling capitalists. Blame the rich and the famous for the country's ills. As bonsai kids, are you concerned that President Xi is cracking down on tech, education, and entertainment and insisting that corporations and billionaires give back more to society? And they did. Tencent and Alibaba each pledged more than $15.5 billion to the common prosperity program, and others like Pinduoduo, Xiaomi, and ByteDance have donated millions to charity.

And why not? These companies' wealth has mushroomed along with China's economic growth. Celebrity fan clubs have become networks of mass mobilization, rallying millions of members to support their idols online with clicks and money. Billionaires are selling books preaching a gospel of self-made success, while Jack Ma, Alibaba cofounder, opened his own elite academy to raise future entrepreneurs.

But now the winds are changing. Celebrities and famous entertainers should promote the traditional Chinese culture. The National Radio and Television Administration is purging celebrities of "fake, ugly and evil values," singling out "sissy idols" or men who wear makeup or act feminine. The warning is out against the influence of big money manipulating the culture and arts in China, against irrational expansion of capital, giving wealthier and middle-class students an unfair edge. Art and literature should serve the common people and socialism. Yes, "it is the return of red, of heroes, of hot-bloodedness." It is like the coming of a second Cultural Revolution. Why not? China can claim success in containing COVID-19 and lifting over eight hundred million people out of poverty.

China gets what China wants. Why not? China is capable of doing things nobody else has ever done.

CHAPTER FORTY-TWO

As bonsai kids, are you worried or concerned that many of your generation are less enthusiastic about marriage? The latest figures from the Ministry of Civil Affairs are showing that the nation's marriage rate has witnessed a continuous decline from 2013. It is obvious that the younger generation has shown less enthusiasm for marriage, though many are yearning for romance and love. In 2013, 13.47 million couples got married. In 2020, that number has dropped to 8.13 million. On the other hand, in 1987, 580,000 couples ended their marriages, and that number rose to 3.73 million in 2020.

Are you concerned that more bonsai kids prefer a later marriage? What dampened the enthusiasm for marriage? Why do so many bonsai kids remain single? There are many reasons for this delay—unaffordable housing prices, high education costs, stronger sense of independence, finding it hard to fall in love, unsociable character, and high standards for potential partners. Don't give up yet because it seems 80 percent in a survey have registered in matchmaking social networks, and 40 percent are working hard to increase their wealth, like owning an apartment, to be more attractive to potential partners.

Chapter Forty-Three

As bonsai kids, are you concerned that the central government is cracking down on the education industry, one way to deal with the rising inequality and skyrocketing costs? One way to reduce the burden on children? One way to adjust what the children are learning? What about removing English and only taking math and Chinese for students from third through fifth grade in Shanghai starting in the fall of 2021? What happens in Shanghai, China's most cosmopolitan city, are indications of things to come elsewhere in the nation; this is the modus operandi used by the communist government throughout its history.

As bonsai kids, are you concerned that the central government is also banning the use of unapproved foreign textbooks in primary and junior high schools and introducing the "Xi Jinping thought" textbook to all schools nationwide in the fall of 2021, one way to instill positive attitude toward the motherland and the Chinese Communist Party?

Is Beijing or the central government genuinely concerned with the cutthroat exam competition requiring young people to study and study all day long, one way to remove the enormous pressure on younger students? Or is the real truth behind the government action to remove the exorbitant costs of after-school cram schools and household tutoring so families could spend the money on having more children? Many families are complaining they could not afford another child while the central government is gravely concerned with the aging population and labor shortage in the nation, removing deliberately the one-child policy in 2016.

Which strategy is more likely to succeed, addressing educational inequality or stubborn low birth rates? Will setting standard tuition rates or overseeing prices or requiring existing tutoring businesses to register as nonprofits address the low birth rates or educational inequality in the nation? Sadly, many parents are not receptive to the new policies of the central government. The truth is those families with high incomes can afford a higher-quality education no matter what the central government is attempting to do with their new policies.

Many people are concerned that the planned reforms may risk undermining the very education system that has driven China's economic growth for decades and could potentially weaken the country's edge in the global race to produce and cultivate talent. For sure, China is not averse to risks. As one professor friend of mine once said to me, "If China could build the Great Wall of China, everything is possible in China."

CHAPTER FORTY-FOUR

Inspired by a book, *China without Blinders* or *La Chine sans œillères* (in defense of modern China), by two French writers, I sat down to compose (for my Facebook) the piece A New Beacon to the World, which I decided to share with a very eloquent, new, and sophisticated Chinese ambassador to the USA; *China Daily* (communist English newspapers in China, to which I had penned a piece or two while a visiting professor there); and CGTN, China's international TV network. And why not? My roots are in China, and I am Chinese to the marrows of my bones, from head to toe. Nothing could be more authentic. I am proud to be a Chinese.

In around 1903, Grandpa and his growing family immigrated to Malaya (now Malaysia). My grandparents hailed from Fujian Province, China, where Pres. Xi Jinping spent over two decades of his formative life as a top government official on his way to the top leadership post within the CCP. And little did I know that Xiamen University, where I first taught, was about four hours away from Grandpa's enormous tomb in Fuqing, next door to Fuzhou. Like many patriotic Chinese then, Grandpa would often return to mainland China to visit friends and relatives and a daughter, who remained in China because she was adopted by Grandpa's friend. Aunt was a Christian, difficult to believe in communist China, and I had the pleasure to meet her children and grandchildren during my seven eventful years in China.

A NEW BEACON TO THE WORLD

Western politicians and journalists,
To Xinjiang they have never been.
So claim Maxime Vivas and Jean-Pierre Page
In *China without Blinders*, a book they wrote,
La Chine sans œillères in French.
From sixteen international experts and scholars,
Their knowledge in economics, history,
Diplomacy, immunology,
Tibetan studies, and journalism,
Like mighty weapons,
Vivas and Page sought to use,
To tear down walls
Of Western misconceptions about China.

Western politicians and journalists,
Objective field research they never did.
China without Blinders, a surprise to them,
Like a bomb thrown into the water,
Strong big waves, up it stirred.
Without blinders, they,
Like horses, could see the world more clearly.
Veiled for too long
By dark clouds like
Western arrogance and greed,
Blinded by constant hostility,
Western media and myopic politicians they
created, now
Facing the new reality
They had long avoided.

Western politicians and journalists,
Blinders removed, clearly they could see
1.4 billion living, striving, succeeding Chinese people;

Like the Great Wall of China,
To the whole world, they are now visible.
From decades of fragmentation, underdevelopment,
And poverty, unfounded accusation of spreading COVID-19,
bullied by the West, they silently suffered, endured,
Now unstoppable, marching to technological progress,
Scientific development,
Economic superiority,
World dominance, feared by
Western politicians and journalists.

Depressed by their own increasing anxiety,
America and the West, of their own incompetence,
Experienced recession, violence, polarization
Within their own entities.
Social, cultural, political, economic,
Environmental, supply chain crisis
And the inescapable pandemic
Driving them, these harsh forces, to
The edge of madness, incurable insanity,
Their containment of a rising Dragon failed.
Their scapegoat: China.

Sorry, Western politicians and journalists,
No longer will China kowtow
To you or anyone but
Now marching triumphantly to achieving
Socialism with Chinese characteristics.
So the leadership in China,
From rooftops to rooftops,
Across plains, valleys, mountains, and oceans,
Righteously, arrogantly, and proudly
Now they proclaim.

Socialism with Chinese characteristics,
China dream,
Common prosperity,
National rejuvenation,
Redistribution of education, careers,
Economic opportunities and wealth,
Win-win for all,
So they did.

Down the ages,
Nations and empires
From time immemorial,
Through victories and defeats,
Had their share of glory.
But in the words of a Taoist priest,
"All good things must end."
Maybe it is a mandate from heavens;
It is China's time once again,
The Middle Kingdom.
A beacon to the world, proclaim!

EPILOGUE

Truth be told, I wrote my first book, *For My Hands Only*, the year before I retired from teaching in a public school here in Washington State, USA. I am getting ready to publish my ninth book soon and will work on my tenth book right after that.

When you are old, over fifty or so, in mainland China, you could not help wonder why your grandchildren or adult children think *there is no more sex in your life.* When I first sensed this in China as a visiting professor, I was shameless to confront some of my students and asked them openly why they would think Grandpa or Grandma has given up sex when they reach old age. I said something as stupid as "Come and visit my country, America, and you might be surprised to see many very happy old couples. They are happy because they have a very good sex life." They are still very much in love and behave in public like teenagers in love for the first time. Their bodies and public behavior tell their story. *You will not witness this anywhere in China. Love belongs to the youth.*

My students must be thinking I was a lunatic or someone mentally deranged or unstable. They could not visualize that Grandpa and Grandma could be enjoying sex in bed while they are out somewhere, singing their hearts out at a local karaoke bar outside their campus.

Anyway, like a beggar, I just found some treasure to share with you. I found it in a report in *China Daily*, a major English newspaper of the communist government in China, and I had the privilege to write a thing or two for it when I was a visiting professor in China. It is a story of an incredible man who does what he wants with his life, even though he is now beyond the age of eighty years. Yes, he first created a sensation when he appeared onstage as a male model during Beijing Fashion Week when he was in his late seventies.

Born in 1936 (way before China became a communist country in 1949 or the implementation of the one-child policy in 1980) to a rural family in Shenyang, Liaoning Province (one of the coldest places in northern China), in 1936, Wang Deshun was once a bus conductor, a factory worker, and then a stage actor in 1960 and appeared in bit parts in films. Imagine learning English at the age of forty-four. Many young people do that because they want to see the world or work for multinational companies in China or serve in diplomatic services.

He never stopped pushing the limits. At age fifty, he started fitness training. Then he began riding a horse at sixty-five, riding a motorcycle at seventy-eight, and hitting the catwalk at seventy-nine in the famous Beijing Fashion Week, wowing the audience with his incredibly firm physique. And soon he was dubbed "China's hottest grandpa." You would think that was it. At eighty-five years old in August of 2021, he started flying at Miyun Airport in Beijing (the capital of China) in an SW 100 light aircraft, performing incredible turns and climbs, the oldest person to engage in flight training in mainland China. And because of his excellent physical stats, he was able to apply for a flight license and lucky to have a professional team to customize a personal training plan.

"I've been dreaming of flying for more than fifty years, so I thought I should learn. I thought I could do this," Wang said.

"It's never too old to pursue your dream. Age has never been a hurdle. Just do it," he added.

Wang Deshun continues to challenge himself in his life. If he can do it, I can do it too. There is hope for me and all of us. Yes, you are never too old to pursue your dream.

Wang Deshun represents the best of China. He is China. And he is the perfect role model for all bonsai kids in China today. If he can do it, I can do it too.

ACKNOWLEDGMENTS

Thanks to many friends, colleagues, and former students in mainland China for their kindness and generosity in allowing me and guiding me to understand the seriousness of the one-child policy (1980 to 2016) and how it affected and continues its influence on their lives and those of their families, relatives, coworkers, and students of today and the nation.

Thanks to Mary Pu and Jake Chen for sharing their photos for the cover of the book. My special thanks to Dr. Chen Chao for designing the cover.